Words from Jesus

Bible Lessons to Increase Your Faith

Written By: Debra Albrecht

Words From Jesus

Bible Lessons to Increase Your Faith

Copyright © 2023 by Debra Albrecht

First Edition

Pure thoughts Publishing, LLC

www.purethoughtspublishing.com

ISBN: 978-1-953760-31-9

Pure Thoughts Publishing LLC

Table of Contents

All scripture is given by inspiration of God, and is profitable for doctrine, for reproof, for correction, for instruction in righteousness: That the man of God may be perfect, thoroughly furnished unto all good works.

II Timothy 3:16-17 (KJV)

1

Alone

Alone – *separated from others; without aid or support*

The word 'alone' comes from a combination of "all" and "one". Time spent alone with someone who is a close friend is vital to building a relationship. The stronger the relationship the more alone time has been invested with the other person. A few years back, my work took me on a project out of town. A coworker went along with me to help with the work. She and I spent quite a bit of alone time both in our travel and in our evenings after the work ended each day. I was able to ask her questions that I normally wouldn't ask anyone on an average work day. I began to see and understand parts of her personality that I wouldn't have seen in a professional environment. I found it to be the beginning of a relationship I rarely have with fellow workers. Jesus desires to have a deep and meaningful relationship with every one of us. He is there waiting to spend some quality alone time with you. Too many times we can't see Jesus anticipating and desiring to spend time with us because we are busy with many things. Luke tells us of the account of Martha receiving Jesus into her house.

> Luke 10:39-42. And she had a sister called Mary, which also sat at Jesus' feet, and heard His word. But Martha was

cumbered about much serving, and came to Him, and said, Lord, dost thou not care that my sister hath left me to serve alone? Bid her therefore that she help me. And Jesus answered and said unto her, Martha, Martha, thou art careful and troubled about many things: But one thing is needful; and Mary hath chosen that good part, which shall not be taken away from her.

Martha was anxious about all the hospitality arrangements. She wanted to make sure all the food was ready at the same time, that the house was neat and everything was in its place. Not to be forgotten was that she needed to clean herself up and make sure she was presentable. She kept going over her list to make sure she hadn't forgotten anything. Don't forget, this was Jesus, the Messiah coming to their home. Everything had to be perfect.

Can you tell by how I described her, that I know Martha very well because I would act the same way? The scripture says that Martha also sat at Jesus' feet. She found time to sit and listen to Jesus teach between getting up and making sure everyone was taken care of. She was the ultimate hostess. But her sister, Mary, wasn't concerned about any of those things. In fact, she quit helping Martha two days ago. She was already cleaned and dressed long before Jesus got there. As soon as He arrived, she sat down at His feet and listened to Him teach, something she loved to do. Mary chose the good part- that alone time at Jesus' feet. She didn't care if the food was ready or even if it was burnt to a crisp, she just wanted to hear Jesus. She knew this was the food she needed to feed her spirit and she was showing Jesus just how much their relationship meant to her. It is easy in our everyday lives to get caught up in being encumbered or distracted with too much care about things. Many times, we assume, like Martha, that all of this busyness in serving is just what Jesus wants. He didn't ask us to sacrifice our fellowship time with Him to take care of others, that is His responsibility. He didn't ask you to fill your schedule with works and fail to spend quality alone time with Him. I am not saying that we shouldn't do works, but there comes a time when we need to lay works aside and focus on our relationship with Jesus. The one thing that is needful is sitting alone with Him at His feet and hearing His word. Sitting at His feet represents a spirit of submission in us and our trust in Him. This is the good part and cannot be taken away from us. Your relationship with Jesus is not all about you talking to Him, praying with requests you have, and even including praises to God for what He has done. But there also must be some time allowed for the Lord to speak to you. How many of you take time to sit quietly, to listen to what the Holy Spirit is saying into your spirit? How long can you do it until you are thinking about what you will cook for supper, what you read on social media today that upset you, or maybe what you are going to pray next when it is your turn to speak? In a healthy relationship, communication goes two ways, with each side hearing and absorbing what the other person is saying. This trait must be developed for the relationship to be nourished.

The enemy would like you to believe that you are alone in every trial and tribulation you go through. That no one else has gone through what you are going through. If you don't have Jesus in your life with the indwelling of the Holy Spirit, then you are alone in your troubles. But when you walk alone with Jesus by your side, there is nothing you cannot walk through. There is only one who's council we should require. That of Jesus Christ - Him alone. And He will be there for us.

Sometimes, if it wasn't for Jesus walking with us, we would have never made it through the tests and trials in our lives. The first time I brought forth this word was October 3, 2016. At that time, my husband and I had been married 43 years. We had ups and downs in our relationship, but we were always there for each other. He was my spiritual warrior, a rock of strength I depended on.

Ten days after I wrote this word, my husband went home to be with Jesus in his sleep. The Holy Spirit had prepared my heart for his passing. Earlier, in the spring of that year, God spoke into my heart that someone close to me would be passing away soon. Then one day a poem came across my computer, and it ministered to me. It described exactly what happened that night. God closed Phil's eyes and took him home. The last step in my preparation was God speaking to me in this word 'alone', telling me I wouldn't walk this path He has for me by myself. I definitely missed my husband, but I knew it was the will of God for his life. There were so many decisions to be made the first few months and there were nights spent on my knees in tears before God, praying for guidance and strength to go on. In my mind, I felt like I needed someone physically here to help me. I reached out to friends for advice and Jesus shut those doors. He told me – I am your husband now and will be that spiritual warrior, that rock you can depend on. And He didn't fail me. I am filled with the Holy Spirit with evidence of speaking in tongues and know the power of my prayers in the Spirit. If it hadn't been for that power given to me, I would have had a much harder time making it through. But the strength He gave me in those prayers at that time ministered to friends who commented on how peaceful I was. It was a witness of the faithfulness of God to each of us. In Genesis 2:18(KJV) God said – It is not good that man should be alone; I will make him an help meet for him. We have all heard it preached that this help meet was the woman, as a companion. But Jesus sent us a greater one to walk along side of us. In John 15:26 Jesus tells His disciples that when He leaves, He will send a Comforter,

One who is called to walk with you, to give you a deeper knowledge of the gospel truth, and the divine strength needed to assist you in going through trials and persecutions. If you are a son of God, filled with the Holy Spirit, you are never alone. He is always there to walk with you.

Hebrews 13:5b(KJV) tells us that Jesus said He will never leave us alone. He will never forsake us. He will be there for you even unto the end of the world. He is waiting to be alone with you, to build that relationship with Him that only comes by being in His presence, sitting at His feet, and hearing His word. He desires to walk with you and talk with you. Jesus is waiting for you.

> Revelation 3:20 – Behold, I stand at the door, and knock: if any man hear My voice, and open the door, I will come in to him. And will sup with him, and he with Me.

Jesus is telling us that He is just outside of our heart, waiting to come in. He would never just barge in, tearing down the door to take over your heart. He is a gentleman and is patiently waiting for an invitation to come in. How often do you have someone knocking at the door of your home that you just leave outside? Do you just leave them there, not knowing what they want? Don't you answer the door to find out why they are there? How much more should we open the door of our hearts to Jesus Christ, the Messiah? The King of Kings and Lord of Lords who wants to come into us. He isn't just coming in to sit down anywhere, but coming in to be near us. The scripture says He will sup with us. He will sit down to eat with us. This action deepens the friendship relationship we have with Him. A meal together is one of the main ways relationships are started, developed, and enjoyed. By answering the door, and allowing Jesus to come into your heart, you are initiating a connection to begin and you will never be alone. In and of myself, I can do nothing, but with Jesus by my side, I can do all things. No one comes to Jesus perfect, but through Him we are made a new creation, by Him we are never alone. He will never leave us nor forsake us. He so wants to build a relationship with each of us, He loves us and died on the cross for our sins. There should be nothing greater in our life than our friendship and communion with Jesus, nothing should be more important than Him. This friendship and communion comes with spending quality time with Him, both in prayer and in reading His Word, the Bible. We should get to the place where not only does our spirit long after time with Him, but our soul desires to have alone time, a one on one with Him.

Don't let the things of this world encumber you and keep you from the good part – Jesus in your life forever.

We give Him all praise and all glory.

2

Gratitude

Gratitude – readiness to show appreciation for and to return kindness

We have grown up with a practice of tipping for services rendered in an act of appreciation. When a waitperson meets your needs and makes your meal pleasantly enjoyable, appreciation is shown by giving them a monetary show of thankfulness with a gratuity. While you, as the customer have full control over the amount of the tip, the result is to show gratitude to the server or anyone who has performed a service for you. We are to be showing this same spirit of gratefulness to Jesus for all He does for us, even when it doesn't appear to be pleasant. When the experience doesn't turn out as our preconceived idea, do we skip a gratuity or, even worse, leave a disgraceful amount, murmuring under our breath about the lack of service? We will find out, as did the children of Israel, murmuring and complaining will just get you wandering in the wilderness for 40 years. They complained about hunger, thirst and even of giants in the promised land. From the time they left Egypt until they were about to step into the promised land, they continually voiced their opinion negatively about their conditions. Each time they fought against God; Moses stood in the gap for them. The children of Israel had been led to the border of the promised land, but instead of being grateful to God for bringing them out of their captivity and grateful to Moses for leading them, they murmured and complained.

> Numbers 14:1-4(KJV) – And all the congregation lifted up their voice, and cried; and the people wept that night. And all the children of Israel murmured against Moses and against Aaron: and the whole congregation said unto them, Would God that we had died in the land of Egypt! Or would God we had died in this wilderness! And wherefore hath the Lord brought us unto this land, to fall by the sword, that our wives and our children should be a prey? Were it not better for us to return into Egypt? And they said one to another, Let us make a captain, and let us return into Egypt.

The children of Israel decided that the position they were in could not possibly be where God would have them. They felt that their leader (Moses) had led them astray and surely there was someone who could lead them in a better way. As a nation, have we not been found murmuring and complaining about what is happening among our leaders? Instead of being grateful for the opportunity to pray and seek God for the will of this nation and our leaders, we continue to find fault by grumbling. But we are told there is a better way. We should accept that God has a plan for us and would not leave us nor forsake us. However, He will not tell us what His plan is, rather we should believe that whatever His will for us is going to be, will be in our best interest.

> Psalms 27:13(KJV) – I had fainted, unless I had believed to see the goodness of the Lord in the land of the living.

There is goodness in our nation. You must believe that you will see it. You must have the faith of God to know you have the eyes to see what He is doing for us. Looking for God's goodness has to be a concerted effort for each of us. It may be in something as insignificant as a snowstorm. Being able to sit indoors and watch the big beautiful white snowflakes fall silently to the earth and coat the ground. Those that are of a complaining spirit would say the snow makes it hard to drive or is so wet and cold. But if you look at it from the goodness of the Lord, you will see the promise that we have been given in Isaiah.

> Isaiah 55:10(KJV) – For as the rain cometh down, and the snow from heaven, and returneth not thither, but watereth the earth, and maketh it bring forth and bud, that it may give seed to the sower, and bread to the eater:

So, don't be swayed by your circumstances. Have a good time through this. Our joy should be in the Lord. Being grateful in all that He does and, in all things, give thanks. Don't respond by complaining. Do not let that come near you. Do not fall to that but be a grateful person. Only by being grateful, thankful and full of gratitude can we shine as lights to all those around us.

> Philippians 2:13-15(KJV) – For it is God which worketh in you both to will and to do of His good pleasure. Do all things without murmurings and disputings: That ye may be blameless and harmless, the sons of God, without rebuke, in the midst of a crooked and perverse nation, among whom ye shine as lights in the world.

God is energizing you so you can do what pleases Him. Don't grumble, don't even have secret displeasure or doubtful reasoning. With an attitude full of thanksgiving, you will be found innocent and blameless. As a son of God, you have been called to live without sin or stain among a nation of people who can only see the bad in things, continually murmuring and complaining. With gratitude in your heart to God, you will shine as a light to those around you. Daily we should look for opportunities to be grateful to God for His working in our life. In our prayers, we should be giving thanks for each of His promises He has fulfilled in our life that day. In everything give thanks: for it is God's will in Christ Jesus for each of us.

We give Him all praise and all glory.

3

Listen

Listen – to give one's attention to a sound in order to hear what is being said.

It is an awesome privilege to stand in the presence of our Father, and to have Him speak into our lives. But do we have the ears to hear what He is saying to us? The dictionary tells us listening is giving attention to a sound. But the Hebrew word for listen, hear, or hearken takes it a little further than that. To listen in the Bible means to hear intelligently, with an implication of obedience. Not only are you giving your attention to what our Father is saying to you, but you are acknowledging it as coming from Almighty God, you accept it as His word in you and will be obedient to do whatever He speaks to you. In order to hear His voice, you must have ears to hear. Jesus tells us in John about those who hear His voice.

> John 10:24-27(KJV) – Then came the Jews round about Him, and said unto Him, How long dost thou make us to doubt? If thou be the Christ, tell us plainly. Jesus answered them, I told you, and ye believed not: the works that I do in my Father's name, they bear witness of Me. But ye believe not, because

ye are not of my sheep, as I said unto you. My sheep hear my voice, and I know them, and they follow Me:

Jesus was walking through the temple in Jerusalem and some of the Jews gathered around Him, asking "If you are The Christ, tell us plainly." Jesus' reply was, I told you and you do not believe. You do not believe because you are not my sheep. You do not listen. You lack faith because you are not My sheep. My sheep know My voice, are acquainted with the sound of My voice, and respond when they hear My voice. How do we know how to hear the voice of the Lord? Is there a special place we need to go to hear Him? Elijah was seeking to hear from the Lord for his life and ran into the desert to find solitude. These are the instructions that came from God.

> I Kings 19:11-13(KJV) And He said, Go forth, and stand upon the mount before the LORD. And, behold, the LORD passed by, and a great and strong wind rent the mountains, and brake in pieces the rocks before the LORD; but the LORD was not in the wind: and after the wind an earthquake; but the LORD was not in the earthquake: and after the earthquake a fire: and after the fire a still small voice. And it was so, when Elijah heard it, that he wrapped his face in his mantle, and went out, and stood in the entering in of the cave. And, behold, there came a voice unto him, and said, What doest thou here, Elijah?

In these scriptures, Elijah was being pursued by Jezebel's soldiers to be killed, so he was seeking God for his protection. God directed Elijah to go stand on the mountainside in His presence. A great wind came and separated the mountains and crumbled every stone, but the Lord was not in the wind. Then an earthquake shook the whole earth, but the

Lord was not in the earthquake. Finally, there was a fire, but the Lord was not in the fire. It does not say God told Elijah that each of these occurrences was caused by Him. The scripture says the Lord was not in them. The Lord was in the breeze that blew on Elijah. Jesus wants to speak to us, but He is not speaking in the wind, an earthquake or a fire. He desires to speak to us in a still small voice. But in order to hear this voice, we must first calm our souls, turn off all the voices in our heads, and open our ears to hear and our hearts to believe. How can you listen(hear) if you are not quiet enough to hear the voice of Jesus? You will not hear Jesus speak through your natural ears. He doesn't speak into our brains but into our hearts. We need to sit still, turn off everything inside of us, and be sensitive to His voice however He chooses to speak to us.

Scripture tells us we are to desire the gifts of the Spirit, but in order to do this, we must have ears to hear what Jesus is saying. To prophesy, you have to believe in your heart that He speaks to you and you hear Him. What does your heart tell you? There is so much He wishes to share with us, but our ears must be open and our heart has to believe. It is difficult to believe what you have not heard and it is difficult to walk in what you have not heard. But this is not because Jesus has not said it, it is because you have not heard it. Our prayer should be that the ears and eyes of our heart are open to everything Jesus is telling us this day. It is crucial that we be able to hear the Master's voice in the coming days. Hearing from the Lord allows our nature to align with His. Hearing from the Lord is seeking Him and then waiting for His word. The more you draw near to the Lord, the more you will hear. There are so many voices trying to fill us with false information. The only way we will be able to navigate through all the voices coming against us is to know the voice of our Shepherd and to follow it. Be sensitive to His voice, sit still, turn off everything inside of you and be obedient to what Jesus says.

We give Him all praise and all glory.

4

Long-suffering

Long-suffering - *uncomplaining, tolerant, having or showing patience in spite of troubles*

Galatians 5:22-23(KJV) - But the fruit of the Spirit is love, joy, peace, long-suffering, gentleness, goodness, faith, meekness, temperance: against such there is no law.

The result of God's presence within us brings forth fruit; much the same way that fruit appears in an orchard. This list of fruit is not something you can produce yourself – the Spirit of God manifests them in you. We are familiar with most of the fruits mentioned in these scriptures, but long-suffering is not a word commonly used in conversation these days. Long-suffering is not simply suffering for a long time, but it means to patiently endure wrongs or difficulties. It is not patience, but to patiently endure. We have situations happen in our lives every day that come to steal our joy, love, and peace. You are driving down the highway, singing along with the praise music coming from the speakers and the car driving in the lane beside you decides he wants in your lane and cuts you off. What is your reaction? Do you endure long-suffering, continuing to praise God or do you give that driver a piece of your mind even though he can't hear you? I'm not talking about allowing people to walk all over you. But there are situations that happen in your life that you can't change, that will steal your peace, your love, and your joy. There is nothing you can do to change what that driver did to you; the only one that has been affected is you.

Have you ever thought about the long-suffering God goes through with each of us? He already knows the outcome of our lives; He is the Alpha and the Omega. Still, He patiently endures all the mistakes we make, all the wrong turns we take, all the stumbles we go through. He doesn't yell at you if you get in His way and end up out of His will. He patiently endures.

> Romans 9:22-23(KJV) – What if God, willing to shew his wrath, and to make His power known, endured with much long-suffering the vessels of wrath fitted to destruction: and that He might make known the riches of His glory on the vessels of mercy, which He had afore prepared unto glory,

God has shown tremendous restraint with each and every one of us, His vessels that are cracked and shattered. Being our Creator, our potter, does He not have the right to show His fury and power when we mess up and smash His vessels into bits? When we don't turn out exactly as planned, does He still not show His mercy to each of us? God is our example of how we should allow the fruit of longsuffering to be a witness in our walk with Him. Those around us should see the testimony in our lives. Don't take lightly the trials you go through, but seek the wisdom of the Lord Jesus Christ for your life as you endure. In His timing, He will use your testimony to speak to one of His.

Several years ago, my husband, Phil, passed away. Jesus had told me eight months before he passed on, that Phil was going to die that year.

I never told Phil about what Jesus had told me. How do you tell someone you have loved for 43 years that he was going to die shortly? How do you endure going through each day without your best friend? I patiently endured those months, waiting for the day of the Lord when He would take Phil away. Looking back when it happened, my heart was so prepared that I could calmly handle all the details that needed to be taken care of at that time. There were no sobbing hysterics as my testimony at the memorial service and the fellowship afterward was of the keeping power of the Lord in my life. I saw the hand of God in each decision, each direction for my life and even today, it still amazes me. There was nothing I could do to change the difficulties and situations that came into my life, but I could endure through God's mercy. Since then, God uses my testimony of what He did for me to witness to others. When anyone would say, "Oh, I'm sorry" when I told them Phil had passed, I could tell them about the goodness of the Lord during that time. There have been several women that I have been able to tell of the keeping power of Jesus to give them hope in their situation.

All of us have something to contribute to someone's life. There is something that is etched in our souls that God uses when we are around other people. Through the difficult experiences in life that you have been through, you can teach other people in a deeper way, because of the things that you have been through. We all have treasures in earthen vessels of experiences you have been through and the people God puts in front of you, He wants them to draw upon what you have walked out. So, don't take lightly the longsuffering you go through in your walk with God. What brings you through to the other side ends up being your testimony.

II Corinthians 3:2(KJV) – Ye are our epistle written in our hearts, known and read of all men:

The fruit of long-suffering in our life will be the epistle, the testimony that will be seen and read by all those who come into contact with us. Hebrews 10 admonishes us to consider one another to provoke unto love and to good works. We should think carefully about how to inspire each other to greater love and to righteous deeds, how inventive we can be in encouraging love and helping others. God has patiently endured with each of us. How more should we have long-suffering for those around us?

We give Him all praise and all glory.

5

Humble

Humble – subdue into subjection, bend the knee

I have a small sign on my desk that says "Don't presume to go up". It is there to remind me I am not as important as I think I am. Sometimes it is easy to think more highly than we ought and become puffed up with ourselves. As a child, I felt like there was nothing I couldn't do. When my mother would try to help me, I would tell her; "I can do it myself, mommy". This attitude has carried over into my adult life. But I find that if I continue in that way of thinking, I miss what Jesus would have for me. By bending my knee, subjecting myself, and accepting His will for me, I am able to complete His purpose in every situation. How many of you have walked into an assembly and without asking the Holy Spirit to direct you to where you were to sit, picked out the place of honor you wanted for yourself? Who knows, maybe you were to sit at the back of the assembly next to a person who you would lead to the infilling of the Holy Spirit with evidence by speaking in tongues before the meeting was over. Or maybe you would sit at a table, not knowing that the next table over was an important contact for your business that would bring great blessings to you, or maybe be just the helper you needed to complete a project. Then there is the time that you sat in the back row and someone from the front row came back and escorted you to sit in the front row with them, in a place of honor. If we are subject to the Spirit within us, there is no chance happening in our walk and everything is ordered by the Lord.

> Luke 14:7-11(KJV) - And He put forth a parable to those which were bidden, when he marked how they chose out the chief rooms; saying unto them, When thou art bidden of any man to a wedding, sit not down in the highest room; lest a more honourable man than thou be bidden of him; and he that bade thee and him come and say to thee, Give this man place; and thou begin with shame to take the lowest room. But when thou art bidden, go and sit down in the lowest room; that when he that bade thee cometh, he may say unto thee, Friend, go up higher: then shalt thou have worship in the presence of them that sit at meat with thee. For whosoever exalteth himself shall be abased; and he that humbleth himself shall be exalted.

In these scriptures, Jesus was invited to an official's home for a meal. This fellow was a ruling Pharisee leader and the religious groups were closely watching all Jesus' activities. Jesus observed the guests were trying to get the honorable places. During this time, there were no large banquet halls or church fellowship halls to have the weddings and receptions. So, the family home was used for the ceremony and wedding meal. Being that many people were invited, it took several rooms of the house to seat everyone. The main room was reserved for the wedding party, along with the immediate family. Then each subsequent room would have tables for the remaining wedding guests. Those who came that were mere acquaintances were to sit in the room furthest from the main room. Jesus is telling the guests at the dinner it is better to sit in the lowest room and be asked to move up than it is to sit at the main table and be embarrassed when you are asked to move to a lower table. Don't presume to go up. For all those who desire honor shall be brought low; and those who humble themselves will be lifted up. Humbleness is an attitude of the heart, but there is also action with it. There is a bending of the knee with the direction of someone else in our lives; showing a consciousness of one's defects or shortcomings and recognizing the Master. Get down on your knees before Him; it's the only way you'll get on your feet.

James 4:10(KJV) – Humble yourselves in the sight of the Lord, and He shall lift you up.

Have we done what we wanted and then asked God to bless it or have we bent the knee and come into subjection to the mighty hand of God? If we keep our eyes on God and not on ourselves, doing as the Spirit leads in our lives, doors will be opened and the way will be made for Him to work in our lives. In the natural, humbleness is considered a form of weakness and it is rarely a virtue that our culture values. We are trained from an early age to show our strengths and hide our weaknesses. Peter wrote in his letter:

I Peter 5:5-6(KJV) - Likewise, ye younger, submit yourselves unto the elder. Yea, all of you be subject one to another, and be clothed with humility: for God resisteth the proud, and giveth grace to the humble. Humble yourselves therefore under the mighty hand of God, that He may exalt you in due time.

Peter is quoting a scripture from Proverbs in this letter that tells us that our enemy desires to consume us, but we can find strength to resist him when we depend upon God for His strength. It is not all about you. Jesus desires to use each of us to build His church and He can only do that if we submit, take on a spirit of humility, and humble ourselves. God is opposed to and resists those with a prideful spirit. It is important for us to realize that we don't bring any goodness to God. No, God brings it all to you. Don't presume to go up.

We give Him all praise and all glory.

6

Anxious

Anxious – experiencing worry, unease, or nervousness, typically about an imminent event or something with an uncertain outcome.

Before I begin with this word, let me admonish those who are saying to themselves, "I'm not anxious. I trust in Jesus to take care of everything in my life. This word is for someone else." Well, when Jesus started dealing with me on this word, those were the thoughts that went through my mind. I felt like everything was under control and I had turned all my cares over to God. It's amazing how at times like these, situations occur that show you just how anxious and nervous you can become. And depending on your response to the anxiety is an indicator of how much of God's peace you have in your heart.

> Philippians 4:6-7(KJV) - Be careful for nothing; but in everything by prayer and supplication with thanksgiving let your requests be made known unto God. And the peace of God, which passeth all understanding, shall keep your hearts and minds through Christ Jesus.

Paul is telling the church in Philippi not to be full of care for anything but prayer. Just pray. Don't discuss all your worries and fears with those around you. Don't fret over situations that are out of your control. Pray about everything, your worries should be prayers of praise, turning all your concerns over to God. Paul is teaching them a lesson Jesus taught in Matthew 6:31(KJV) – Take no thought. Don't look at what is going on around you. Recently I had an occasion that anxiousness rose its ugly head in my life. I fell and busted my lip. It bled profusely and I knew by looking at it that if I didn't get it taken care of, my smile would never be the same. My dilemma was do I allow it to heal by itself and have an ugly scar or do I get medical attention? Time was of the essence in this decision, but that didn't make it any easier to feel like I had the answer. Do I leave it? Or do I go to the emergency room? I prayed for wisdom and the Spirit instructed me to call a prayer warrior, someone who would give me Godly counsel, as I didn't have the mind of Christ for the situation. I called and by the Holy Spirit I heard, "Go to the hospital and get it taken care of." In looking back at the situation, I can see the hand of God in directing me to the correct facility, with the correct doctor, so the peace of God that is beyond all of my human understanding filled me and settled my anxiety. I learn that the circumstances of my life do not affect His Kingdom. There is nothing that will happen to me He doesn't already know; God is still in control of everything. Therefore, Jesus is teaching – Take no thought. It is in the mind, the thought realm, that the spirit of anxiousness and worry come over us.

II Corinthians 10:5(KJV) – Casting down imaginations, and every high thing that exalteth itself against the knowledge of God, and bringing into captivity every thought to the obedience of Christ.

We should take control of every reasoning or argument, every emotion which rises up in our imaginations that is not of God. Every worry, fret, or anxious feeling begins with our mind, creating a thought that sets itself up against the true knowledge of God. We should be in a place in our walk with Jesus where we deal with the thought. How do we take no thought if every time we quit thinking about one worry, another one creeps in? We pray in the Spirit, shutting down our minds. We speak His Word into our lives, the promises He has made to us. In doing so, our mind is taken off the cares of the world and placed on God.

Isaiah 26:3(KJV) – Thou wilt keep him in perfect peace, whose mind is stayed on Thee: because he trusteth in Thee.

With so much turmoil in our world today, it is difficult to keep our minds from straying to what is going on around us. If we focus on this unrest, it can cause our mind to wander to thoughts that are filled with all kinds of anxiety, worry, and fear. Jesus said, Take no thought. Remove anything from your life that speaks gloom and fear. Speak the Word of God into your life by reading His word out loud. Allow Him to fill you with His perfect peace because you have put your trust in Him for your life. This is not a onetime process. This should be done continually as you are constantly bombarded with thoughts that will bring you down. When the peace of God leaves you, know that anxiousness is trying to take over. Pray. Pray about everything, your worries should be prayers of praise, turning all your concerns over to God. And the peace of God will keep your heart and mind through Christ Jesus.

We give Him all praise and all glory.

7

Habitation

Habitation – *to live in a particular place, a house or a home*

We have the privilege to live in a time when we are able to have a personal relationship with Jesus Christ. Those living during the Old Testament period of the bible had to go to the temple to find the presence of God. We don't have to go to a church building or a temple constructed of man's hands to be in the presence of the Most High God. All we have to do is say the name of Jesus and He is right there with us. We become one with Him. The habitation of the Holy Spirit is one who is called out. As I Corinthians 1:9(KJV) says we are called unto the fellowship of His Son Jesus Christ our Lord. Paul wrote to the church at Corinth in his letter –

> I Corinthians 6:19-20(KJV) – What? Know ye not that your body is the temple of the Holy Ghost which is in you, which ye have of God, and ye are not your own? For ye are bought with a price: therefore, glorify God in your body, and in your spirit, which are God's.

Paul was reminding them that the Holy Spirit, which comes from God, dwelled within them. Paul preached that you don't own yourself, you have been purchased with the precious blood of Jesus and made His own. Your body is the home of the Holy Spirit that was given to you, and He lives within you. We are to use every part of our body to give glory back to God because He owns it.

Over 30 years ago, when I received the baptism of the Holy Spirit with evidence of speaking in tongues, Jesus told me our home would be a habitation of shepherds. Thinking at the time of what it meant, I took the words in a literal sense and thought the structure we lived in would be filled with ministers coming to stay. Phil and I had just moved into a home that was large enough to accommodate plenty of company. We knew several ministers that traveled to the DFW area to hold meetings at the time and we invited them to stay with us. For the next 25 years, we lived there having very few people ever stay with us. I have since realized that the habitation of shepherds Jesus was speaking about is not in the natural as in my home, the building I live in, but in the spiritual where He comes to dwell with me. The Holy Spirit dwells within me. We are a place where the new births in the body of Christ can be ministered to by those who have been sold out to God. Each of us is being built on a solid, firm foundation and joined together stone by stone in Him, creating a sacred dwelling place.

> Ephesians 2:19-22(KJV) – Now therefore ye are no more strangers and foreigners, but fellow citizens with the saints, and of the household of God; and are built upon the foundation of the apostles and prophets, Jesus Christ Himself being the chief corner stone; in whom all the building fitly framed together groweth unto an holy temple in The Lord: in whom ye also are builded together for an habitation of God through the Spirit.

We are no longer outcasts and wanderers, but members of God's own family. We are being built on a foundation of the apostles, prophets and Jesus Christ. We are temples of the living God in earthen vessels, being fitly joined together. In I Peter 2:5(KJV) it says; Ye also, as lively stone, are built up a spiritual house, an holy priesthood, to offer up spiritual sacrifices, acceptable to God by Jesus Christ. We are to present ourselves as building stones for construction. When you think about building a stone wall in the garden, you don't start with the smallest stone laid on the bottom and gradually use the larger ones as you build the wall up. If in doing so, your wall will surely collapse and tumble over. The experienced stone mason picks out the largest, heaviest, sturdiest stones to lay the foundation for his stone wall. These are stones that have not allowed wind, water and time to erode them down, but have endured the test of time. These are stones that will hold up the weight of all the other stones that are being built on them. The foundational stones will have traits of love, acceptance, healing, protection, instruction, comfort, and correction. These qualities are what the smaller stones need to assist them in growing into larger stones to put greater strength on the stone wall. Those who have been called out will need these characteristics to minister to wounded saints coming out of the buildings constructed with the hands of man. Jesus is building His church. He is looking for foundational stones, those who have endured. Now is the time to get into the presence of Jesus for wisdom and knowledge concerning your place as a stone in His church. If the hand of God is evident in your life, you have something to give to those stones that are coming up. We are all called to be the least in order to be the greatest. In order for Jesus to consider us as a foundational stone, we need to be qualified and trustworthy, have a kingdom mindset, and humble ourselves to be like Him. Is Jesus able to manifest Himself through you and in you? He doesn't dwell in buildings. We are called to be His dwelling place, His habitation on this earth. In order for this to happen you must seek Him out.

> II Corinthians 6:16b(KJV) – ...for ye are the temple of the living God; as God hath said, I will dwell in them, and walk in them; and I will be their God, and they shall be my people.

We, the ones who are called out, are the home of the living God. We desire to be where He dwells, where His presence is. This happens by seeking His face and allowing Him to come into you and manifest Himself through you. He desires to use every one of us, but that can only be done if you become His place of habitation. Seek Him while He may be found.

We give Him all praise and all glory.

8

Bridegroom

Bridegroom – *a man on his wedding day or just before and after the event.*

When I started praying about this word, I was reminded of how last names came into existence. In the Middle Ages, small villages were separated by large areas of farmlands and people rarely met those from other areas. They knew all the other people who lived in their village, so there wasn't a need for last names. But as the villages grew and people traveled more, there became a need to easily identify those they met. One way surnames or last names were created was by identifying them as their fathers' children; such as a father named John might have a son named Stephen. Stephen may have gone by the name Stephen Johnson. My last name is German meaning novel, bright and was originally a given or first name. With this same principle, when you look at the word bridegroom, it breaks down to be the groom of the bride. The meaning of the word groom is to prepare or make ready someone for a particular purpose or activity. In the New Testament, the word bridegroom is rarely used to identify a particular man on his wedding day. Instead, the word bridegroom is used in reference to the relationship between Jesus and

His body. We find a commonly used scripture describing the bride and the bridegroom in Matthew.

> Matthew 25:1(KJV) – Then shall the kingdom of heaven be likened unto ten virgins, which took their lamps, and went forth to meet the bridegroom.

Here, Jesus is on the Mount of Olives, teaching His disciples privately to picture the kingdom of heaven this way. Ten virgin, unmarried daughters took their lamps and went out to meet the bridegroom. In a procession, the bridegroom and his friends brought the bride from her father's house to his house, where the wedding feast was prepared. Five of the daughters were thoughtless, careless, and foolish while five were practical, sensible, and wise. The foolish ones took no oil for their lamp and the wise ones arrived with plenty of oil for their lamp. All ten daughters arrived at the bridegroom's house before it was prepared and had to wait, so they nodded off and fell asleep. Finally, when all was ready, the cry was heard, Behold, the bridegroom cometh; go ye out to meet him. But the foolish virgins were not allowed into the feast as they had no oil in their lamps, they were not prepared. Do you have oil in your lamp? Are you filled with the Holy Ghost with evidence of speaking in tongues, prepared to meet the bridegroom, Jesus Christ? Paul wrote a very good example of the worthy bride.

> Ephesians. 5:25-27(KJV) – Husbands, love your wives, even as Christ also loved the church, and gave Himself for it; that He might sanctify and cleanse it with the washing of water by the word, that He might present it to Himself a glorious church, not having spot, or wrinkle, or any such thing; but that it should be holy and without blemish.

In this we see that Jesus' love for those who are called out is deep, pure, and sacrificial; the greatest love known to man. We know He gave Himself up completely to make us His own, washing us clean of all our impurities with the powerful presence of His word. He is the groom for His bride, preparing and making ready for a particular purpose; which is to present us unstained, unwrinkled, and unblemished; holy, blameless, and innocent before Him. By the indwelling of the Holy Spirit, we are prepared, cleansed, washed by the spoken word of God, and made into His image to be presented as a bride before Him. No imperfections of any kind. We are transformed by the renewing of our minds, preparing ourselves for His presence.

Let's imagine we are back in the Middle Ages and you are now in need of a last name. What would yours be? Maybe you are English and you would take the name Rankin, as that was your father's given name. Or maybe your family occupation was forestry, keeper of the forest, and you took the name Woodworth. Or would your last name be Jesus, Son of God, the groomer of the bride in your life? It is time to be changed into the image of God. We should purpose in our hearts every day to grow into all that He has for us. Until you are changed, transformed, and renewed; you will not have oil for your lamp and will be left. Let a resolve settle into your heart that you will become the bride that Jesus is grooming. So, He can present you before Himself, a vessel that is ready for His service.

We give Him all praise and all glory.

9

Shift

Shift – *a slight change in position, direction, or tendency*

Several years ago, I thought I was on the path Jesus had for me. My life was like a basket. All the things Jesus had placed in it were all arranged neatly and in order. Each day I knew what was going to happen in my life because I knew the items in my basket were what Jesus had for me. All of my life my basket has been filled with everything neat and in order. But in a two-week period, suddenly all the items in my basket were tossed in the air and I could see them floating above me. Jesus took hold of my basket, held it in His hands, and tossed everything in it up in the air. Everything that had been so neat and in order; now was floating somewhere up above me and I didn't know which way to turn because all the foundation that was so neatly placed in my life had been thrown out of my reach. Now I found myself holding an empty basket waiting for Jesus to put just the things in it He had for my life. I looked up and saw everything that was in my basket floating above my head, out of my reach. My first instinct was to reach up and yank them back into place. But that was not what Jesus had for my life. Even now, Jesus is still filling my basket with what He has for me. In the natural, there have been a few shifts. Moving from the home I had been living in for over 20 years and taking the structure of having a full-time job out of my life were just a couple of the changes.

In the natural all around us, we can see a shift in many areas. With the pandemic, the entire world has had a shift in the last few years, requiring isolation of people from their loved ones. Our nation and our government have had a swing where our founding fathers wouldn't even recognize it. Our form of gathering for worship and church has been modified where we now can attend online. Also, there is a shift coming in the spiritual. We are being called deeper into the things of the Lord. But this calling is not coming from a preacher or a prophet. This calling is between you and Jesus and you must get before the Father for yourself to hear what He is saying to you. The Father is desiring to cleanse and purify everything out of you that is not of Him. He is looking to mold you into the perfect vessel He desires you to be. In the book of Jeremiah, he had been told by the Lord to speak to the children of Israel concerning idolatry and their rebellious spirit. But Jeremiah knew the people would scoff at him, so he pleaded to God to destroy the people. God speaks this to Jeremiah.

> Jeremiah 18:1-6(KJV) – The word which came to Jeremiah from the Lord, saying, Arise, and go down to the potter's house, and there I will cause thee to hear my words. Then I went down to the potter's house, and, behold, he wrought a work on the wheels. And the vessel that he made of clay was marred in the hand of the potter: so he made it again another vessel, as seemed good to the potter to make it. Then the word of the Lord came to me, saying, O house of Israel, cannot I do with you as this potter? Saith the Lord, Behold, as the clay is in the potter's hand, so are ye in mine hand, O house of Israel.

The original clay vessel was found to be marred meaning to be corrupt or deteriorated, such as we can get if we become lack with our walk in Jesus. When Jeremiah went down to the potter's shop, as he watched the potter work with the clay, he found the clay vessel in the potter's hands had become flawed and unusable. So, the potter started again with the same clay, he didn't throw it away. He crushed and squeezed and shaped it into another vessel that was to his liking. If you read on down in the scriptures, God tells Jeremiah that if God Himself were to declare that He was going to destroy a nation and that nation turned away from its evil, then God would not do away with it. Also, if He were to declare He was going to build up a nation that then ignores His voice, thus committing evil, then God would hold back the good that He had planned for them. God did not change His mind in these scriptures, the changing factor was His people. He was going to destroy the nation that was flawed and unusable and restore it into a new vessel, just like the potter with the clay.

Our Father is looking for vessels of honor to pour out His Spirit upon. Paul wrote in his letter to Timothy about becoming an honorable vessel, one useful to the Master.

> II Timothy 2:20-21(KJV) – But in a great house there are not only vessels of gold and of silver, but also of wood and of earth; and some to honour, and some to dishonour. If a man therefore purge himself from these, he shall be a vessel unto honour, sanctified, and meet for the master's use, and prepared unto every good work.

Paul is writing that some vessels (gold and silver) are used for special occasions which bring respect and reverence; while there are other vessels (wood and clay) that are used for mundane tasks. If a man will clean up his life and purify himself from dishonorable teachings; he can become an honorable vessel. All the doctrines that you were taught in various denominations, plus anything you learned in school, college or was passed down by your parents that was not revealed to you by the Holy Ghost, must be eliminated. Only by getting rid of these ideologies can you become an honorable vessel, consecrated and useful to the Master. Jesus wants anything that is not of Him out of you; anything that is not given to you by the indwelling of the Holy Ghost and has not been revealed to you by any means other than Jesus Christ. It is the desire of Jesus to have vessels of honor to serve Him in the coming days, those who have been through the refining fire to be cleansed of all the doctrines, teachings, thoughts, and ideas that are not of Him. Allow Jesus to examine your heart today and reveal what still needs to be cleansed. The time is coming that His vessels will be used. There is a shift in what God is doing in the earth. Will you be ready? Will you be found as a vessel of gold or silver(one who has been through the refining fire), or are you one of wood or clay(one who will be burned up in the fire)? We are in the potter's hand; allow Him to clean and purify you.

We give Him all praise and all glory.

10

Breastplate

Breastplate – a device worn over the torso to protect it from injury

How many of you were brought up in a Christian denomination that taught you the importance of memorizing scripture? I was trained at an early age to memorize and recite scripture, even though the words I recited had not been made real in my life. One of the first scriptures I learned was Psalms 23. Since I have repeated it so many times, I have caught myself reciting it mindlessly and forgetting where I am halfway through it. Jesus woke me in the middle of the night last night and I started praying "The Lord is my shepherd; I shall not want." The Holy Spirit stopped me at that point and asked if the Lord was really my shepherd, which caused me to ponder on the scripture. I began to realize that many of the scriptures I had memorized have just become words to me and I need to let Jesus make them real in my life and write them on my heart. We have been given a whole book of words that He desires to reveal to us, which only comes with meditating on His word. This holds true to the scriptures in Ephesians that instruct us to put on the whole armor of God. Just reciting the scriptures doesn't make them real to us, not until we get a full grasp on what God is revealing through the scriptures, do they begin to have life. Paul wrote the church in Ephesus about being strong in the Lord and the power of His might and admonishing them.

> Ephesians 6:11-14(KJV) – Put on the whole armour of God, that ye may be able to stand against the wiles of the devil. For we wrestle not against flesh and blood, but against principalities, against powers, against the rulers of the darkness of this world, against spiritual wickedness in high places. Wherefore take unto you the whole armour of God, that ye may be able to withstand in the evil day, and having done all, to stand. Stand therefore, having your loins girt about with truth, and having on the breastplate of righteousness;

Paul went on to describe all the pieces of the armor that were needed for spiritual battle. He was telling the church that the real battles and dangers that will be faced are not against flesh and blood. The battles will be held in the spiritual realm against forces of darkness that stay strategically hidden from view. This still holds true for us today. Consequently, we are not physically putting on the actual pieces of armor, but we are to defend ourselves by wearing spiritual armor. In order to do this, we need to allow the Holy Spirit to reveal what each piece of the armor consists of. Before David in the Old Testament went out to slay Goliath, he went before King Saul.

> I Samuel 17:38-39(KJV) – And Saul armed David with his armour, and he put an helmet of brass upon his head; also he armed him with a coat of mail. And David girded his sword upon his armour, and he assayed to go; for he had not proved it. And David said unto Saul, I cannot go with these; for I have not proved them. And David put them off him.

David was telling King Saul that all of this kingly armor was great, but David didn't know how to use it, and had never tried it out. David didn't have a clear understanding of how to fight when he put on the armor of the king. He wasn't used to it; he was used to slaying enemies with stones. We have been given a kingly armor, but we need to spend time in the presence of God to learn how to use each piece; letting Him reveal His purpose in it. Over history, a typical armed soldier's breastplate was made of copper or chain mail and had the name or crest belonging to whomever the soldier's allegiance was to. Our spiritual breastplate has the name "Jesus" across the front of it. It is worn to cover the vital organs, specifically the heart. In the natural, the heart is the center of our blood delivery system, which provides our body with the oxygen and nutrients it needs. In the spiritual, the heart governs our spirit, where all of our desires come from. The heart is seen as the seat of the will, intellect, and feelings. But why do we need protection for the heart?

Proverbs 4:23(KJV) – Keep thy heart with all diligence; for out of it are the issues of life.

This scripture is saying to watch over and guard your heart, because from a sincere and pure heart comes the good and noble things, which influence everything in your life. As Luke 6 tells us, out of the abundance of the heart, our mouth speaks. Whatever is in our heart comes out in our speech, so if the heart is pure and good, then our witness will be pure and good. One of the first battles we have is the taming of the mouth. But as the Holy Spirit works on our heart, it results in peace, joy, love, and kindness coming out of our mouth.

Now that we have learned the function of the breastplate, let's examine what it is made of. Our spiritual breastplate is not made of

39

copper or chain mail as in days of old. As the scripture in Ephesians states, our breastplate is of righteousness, God's righteousness.

II Corinthians 5:21(KJV) – For He hath made Him to be sin for us, who knew no sin; that we might be made the righteousness of God in Him.

It is through Jesus Christ that we have been made acceptable to God and placed in the right relationship with Him by His gracious lovingkindness. This righteousness is not achieved through anything we have done, it is a gift from God. But in order to stay in this position before Him, we must keep our heart pure and good, having our sins cleansed by Jesus in faith.

II Timothy 2:22(KJV) – Flee also youthful lusts: but follow righteousness, faith, charity, peace, with them that call on the Lord out of a pure heart.

Timothy is telling us to grow up into what we follow, those things that cause a pure heart. Guard your heart from being around those with an impure heart with the right standing you have before God. Ephesians 6 instructed us to put on the whole armor of God, which means that there are times in our walk with Him we don't have it on. By allowing doubt, unbelief, worry, or even fear to enter our hearts, our armor has been removed and we stand in full view of the enemy. Being found with our armor on is the way we stand against the wiles and attacks of the enemy, of which there is no doubt they will come. If we will be found in a state of being morally correct and upright before our Heavenly Father, we will be standing with a breastplate of righteousness over a repentant heart, able to face anything the enemy sends our way.

We give Him all praise and all glory.

11

Brave

Brave – ready to face and endure danger without showing fear, to have courage

In the coming days, the enemy will come out in a greater force against the Body of Christ. There will be voices in your ears telling you that you are not ready to face and endure the danger that is about to come. These voices will fill you with dread and will tell you that you need to be brave to endure the danger, causing you to be filled with fear and worry. But these voices and whispers will not be from God. In the New Testament, we are not told to put on a brave face to cover up our fear. However, there are fifteen times that Jesus or the Holy Spirit told someone to "Fear not". These people were not told to be brave by not showing fear. They were told to cast fear out of their lives, aligning their thoughts with the knowledge of God.

> Isaiah 3:18(KJV) – In that day the Lord will take away the bravery of their tinkling ornaments about their feet, and their cauls, and their round tires like the moon,

This verse in Isaiah is the only place in the Bible where any form of the word brave is found. The definition of the word translates as ornament, as any item that draws beauty to oneself. God is telling the children of Israel that under His judgment they will lose all the things they have that make others notice, desire or envy them, everything that consumed their attention to get attention. The word brave in the Bible has nothing to do with the fearlessness needed to face and endure danger. In our walk with Jesus, bravery could be any doctrine, denomination, or idol that causes attention to be drawn to us and does not line up to the word of God for our life.

Many times, when we are attempting bravery, the word courage comes to mind. In the book of Joshua, the word courage is used seven times in God's instructions to Joshua.

> Joshua 1:6-7(KJV) – Be strong and of a good courage: for unto this people shalt thou divide for an inheritance the land, which I sware unto their fathers to give them. Only be thou strong, and very courageous, that thou mayest observe to do according to all the law, which Moses my servant commanded thee: turn not from it to the right hand or to the left, that thou mayest proper whithersoever thou goest.

The word courage used in these scriptures translates to mean to be alert both physically and mentally. Moses had just died and left Joshua in charge of the Children of Israel. They were getting ready to cross the Jordan River into the Promised Land. I am sure Joshua felt like he had some really big shoes to fill since Moses was no longer there. He was now in charge of taking all the Israelites into the Promised Land, which was a daunting task. Joshua was not only a spiritual leader but a military one, so he understood what God was saying in his life by telling him to be of good courage. As a military man, Joshua knew the importance of listening to the commander-in-chief of the army and following orders. He recognized the significance of the voice of God and the weight it carried in Joshua's life. So, when God said to be strong and of good courage, Joshua knew he was to prepare himself for battle. Not by putting on a brave face thru using words and adornment to try to cover his fear; but to prepare his body to be physically ready for battle. Joshua also had to have his heart ready to hear the directions that God would give, the course that was to be taken to accomplish and carry out God's will for the children of Israel. Throughout the book, Joshua saw the hand of the Lord in every battle and every conflict that was encountered, and the victory of taking the land for the children of Israel. With this revelation becoming real for Joshua's life, he was able to witness to commanders of the men of war who had gone with him.

> Joshua 10:25(KJV) – And Joshua said unto them, Fear not, nor be dismayed, be strong and of good courage: for thus shall the Lord do to all your enemies against whom ye fight.

When it came time for Joshua and the Israelites to fight the king of Jerusalem, the accounts of their victories had proceeded them. So, the king of Jerusalem called on the Amorite kings from four royal cities to join him in fighting against Joshua, the Israelites and the men of Gibeon. The Lord had told Joshua in Joshua 10:8(KJV), Fear them not: for I have delivered them into thine hand; there won't be a man of them stand before thee. The five kings had fled to the safety of a cave when the battle was over. Joshua found them there and brought them out and did as he had been instructed by God to do. His orders to each of his men of war included: fear not – there is nothing to be afraid of here; be not dismayed – don't be intimidated; be strong – to strengthen, sustain and encourage; and be of good courage – to possess the motivation from the heart that enables a person to confront danger and difficulty without fear, but with calmness.

Romans 8:15(KJV) – For ye have not received the spirit of bondage again to fear; but ye have received the Spirit of adoption, whereby we cry Abba, Father.

Paul is writing that we have not received a spirit that returns us to the slavery of fear, but the Spirit we have received adopts us and welcomes us into the Father's family. There is no more place in our lives for fear, we don't have to put on a brave face for the world. We can move out in the realization that Jesus goes before us and makes a way where there seems to be no way. We are not intimidated by the force of the enemy because greater is He who is in me than he who is in the world. We can withstand the wiles of the enemy, because it is God that girds me with strength and makes my way perfect. And finally, we don't move out in ourselves, as we move in the Holy Spirit each day, knowing that we are in the perfect will of God for our lives. We move in courage, knowing the Holy Spirit moves with us each step of the way. So don't put on a brave face at your next trial or battle. It may take a higher level of faith to walk in courage, but the outcome will increase God's faith in you.

We give Him all praise and all glory.

12

Stewardship

Stewardship – *the responsible management of something entrusted to one's attention*

Matthew 25:14–16, 19-21(KJV) - For the kingdom of heaven is as a man travelling into a far country, who called his own servants, and delivered unto them his goods. And unto one he gave five talents, to another two, and to another one; to every man according to his several ability; and straightway took his journey. Then he that had received the five talents went and traded with the same, and made them other five talents. After a long time, the lord of those servants cometh, and reckoneth with them. And so, he that had received five talents came and brought other five talents, saying, Lord, thou deliveredst unto me five talents: behold, I have gained beside them five talents more. His lord said unto him, Well done, thou good and faithful servant; thou hast been faithful over a few things, I will make thee ruler over many things: enter thou into the joy of thy lord.

Jesus was speaking to the disciples here concerning the responsibilities they would be given according to their abilities and providing a picture of the coming reality of the kingdom of heaven. Each disciple would be given at least one task or charge and held accountable for the fruit that was produced. In the parable, the first servant received five talents and while his master was away, he traded with those talents and made an additional five talents. His master was very pleased and rewarded his servant. We also know that there was a servant who received one talent. When the master went on his journey, this servant took his one talent, dug a hole, and hid his lord's money in it. When he had to give an account of the fruit of his talent, he said, "Sir, you have such high standards and will not tolerate recklessness. You demand the best. I hid the money in a secure place because I didn't want to disappoint you." His master was so upset, that he took the one talent away from the servant and gave it to the servant who risked the most. Jesus ended the parable with:

Matthew 25:29(KJV) – For unto every one that hath shall be given, and he shall have abundance: but from him that hath not shall be taken away even that which he hath.

To all of us who have valued the blessings and gifts from God, using them wisely, God will give us abundantly more. But those who have not valued the blessings of God, no matter the size, what they have will be taken away. It is interesting to see that the servant of five talents was found a good steward of what he was given and increased his talents. While the servant with the least amount of talents dug a hole and hid his one talent. Jesus said

Luke 12:48b(KJV) – For unto whomsoever much is given, of him shall be much required: and to whom men have committed much, of him they will ask the more.

As sons of God, we have been given much, and much is being required of us. Much has been entrusted to us, much will be expected of us. I have planted a vegetable garden this year for the first time. Although we are still early in the growing season, I must give daily attention to make sure the tender plants are taking root and beginning to grow. In order to be a good steward of the garden and give it the attention that is needed, I go out and check on it every day. I make sure it has enough water and fertilizer to supply its needs. I check for bugs and critters that might be attacking the sensitive young plants. Then, as new fruit comes forth, I monitor it, making sure it is picked at the height of ripeness. This is much like how we should steward the talents God has placed in our lives, and I am not talking just about monetary items. The qualities of a good steward include:

1. Obedience in doing exactly what is instructed of him to do, no matter how inconsequential.

2. Faithfulness to do all tasks set before him and confident that Jesus will make a way.

3. Accountable in all he has been given but found in a spirit of humility knowing that it is Christ in him that does the work.

4. Considerate of others before himself, not having the spirit of pride because of his position.

There are many areas of our lives that we have been given stewardship over by God. During the last presidential election, Jesus showed me that I wasn't being a good steward of the country I have the privilege of living in.

I Timothy 2:1-2(KJV) - I exhort therefore, that, first of all, supplications, prayers, intercessions, and giving of thanks, be made for all men; for kings, and for all that are in authority; that we may lead a quiet and peaceable life in all godliness and honesty.

Is our country in a quiet and peaceful state? I repented for not being a faithful steward, having not given prayers, interceding, and giving thanks for the freedom and liberty we are afforded in this nation. I had not been praying for those in authority and who rule over us. I had not been accountable for the nation I had been given to live in.

Then I began to look at other areas of my life God has given me stewardship over. Those who are privileged to sit under a ministry where the uncut and unedited word of God is preached are to be counted as stewards of that ministry. The season under such tutors and governors is limited and there will come a time when you will be called to go forth. Be found obedient to make the most of the time you have, paying attention to all that is brought forth and supporting all the needs of the ministry, both financially and interceding for them in prayer. If they have taken the time to teach and instruct you, investing in you, surely you could be found a good steward in where you have been placed.

Jesus has also put us in relationships that we should be a good steward over. Just as in the garden, these relationships should be watered and fertilized, not allowing any bugs to eat up the fruit of the connection. We should be planting seeds in this fertile soil that brings forth fruit, some hundredfold, some sixty-fold, and some thirtyfold, allowing Jesus to minister to all those involved. Don't allow familiarity and casualness to come into the relationship, treat it as a treasure, highly prized and valuable.

We have also been given stewardship over the temple of the Most High God in an earthly vessel. The Spirit of God dwells within us, so we should be conscious of what we allow to come into this vessel. We should desire to be an honorable vessel, both in the physical and the spiritual.

> II Timothy 2:21(KJV) – If a man therefore purge himself from these, he shall be a vessel unto honour, sanctified, and meet for the master's use, and prepared unto every good work.

If we will clean our lives, both how we live and what we let into our spirit, then we can become worthy, righteous vessels and useful to the Master. As scripture tells us in Romans 12:1 (KJV) -that we may present our bodies a living sacrifice, holy, acceptable unto God, which is our reasonable service. Stewardship is a lifestyle and requires the Holy Spirit living in us, to lead us and guide us through each day; making us conscious of each and every opportunity.

We give Him all praise and all glory.

13

Prove

Prove – to demonstrate as having a particular quality or worth.

> Romans 12:2(KJV) – And be not conformed to this world: but be ye transformed by the renewing of your mind, that ye may prove what is that good, and acceptable, and perfect, will of God.

Paul is writing to the church in Rome, telling them to not allow this world to mold them into its own image, and not to be carnally minded. Instead, he exhorted them to be transformed from the inside out by renewing their mind. As a result, they would be able to discern what is God's will for their lives. When we begin our walk with Jesus, we come to Him with a carnal mind, like newborn babes who crave pure spiritual milk. Then, as we read the word of God, pray, seek His face, and sit under tutors and governors; our mind, the way we think and perceive things, is slowly transformed and goes through a thorough change. In the beginning, we desire an instant change, but that is not the way God does things. This renewing comes line upon line, here a little and there a little. God is not a microwave with instant results. One day is with the Lord as a thousand years and a thousand years as one day. So, our transformed mind full of God's revealed word doesn't come instantly and our walk with Jesus is not a marathon, but one step at a time. Once you begin having the spiritual mind instead of the carnal mind, Jesus begins to order your footsteps to take action.

James 1:22(KJV) – But be ye doers of the word, and not hearers only, deceiving your own selves.

The word "doer" in Greek means a performer or an architect of the sayings of God. Put His word into action. If you think hearing matters most, you are going to find you have been deceived. Don't just listen to God's word, you must do what it says. Our testimony should be lived out every day for others to see. Walking out what God tells us to do causes us to get into a closer relationship with Him, taking us from an independent state into one dependent upon Him. When you are walking with someone, you walk in the same direction. If you walk in different directions, you can't talk or listen to them, you can't share things with them. When you walk with Jesus, your will is going to align with His will, as your focus will be on Him and you draw closer to Him. Our desire to have fellowship with Jesus and be like Him will grow, while our worldly desires will decrease. Walking in the will of God for our lives is not an easy thing. First, we start with the major areas in our life. Are you in God's will in the place you live? Is the job you have God's will for your life? Are you in the body of Christ God has planted you in? Then, as Jesus begins to reveal His word to you, other areas of your life will come into alignment with His will.

In the scripture we read in Romans 12, it says with the renewing of your mind, you may prove what is that good, acceptable, and perfect, will of God. The word "prove" in this scripture means to recognize something as genuine after examination and consideration. To verify what is the will of God, we must have spent time walking each day with

Him, talking and listening to Him, getting to know His ways, and not our own. It is our protection in days ahead to walk in the will of the Father for our lives, as we know not what is to come.

> James 4:13-15(KJV) – Go to now, ye that say, To day or to morrow we will go into such a city, and continue there a year, and buy and sell, and get gain: whereas ye know not what shall be on the morrow. For what is your life? It is even a vapour, that appeareth for a little time, and then vanisheth away. For that ye ought to say, If the Lord will, we shall live, and do this, or that.

We don't even know the least thing that will happen in our lives tomorrow, much less the major things. What in your life is secure? In a puff of smoke, everything in your life could vanish, so you can't rely on it. All we can rely on is, if we are in the will of God for our lives, He will take care of us. If you will notice, in Romans 12:2 it says what is that good, and acceptable, and perfect will of God. So, we are able to walk in the good will of God for our life, walk in the acceptable will of God for our life, and walk in the perfect will of God for our life. Jesus showed me this morning as I was working in the garden, on one of the tomato plants I was getting ready to harvest, the difference between them. The green tomatoes are those that have not been on the vine long enough and are not yet ripened. This is the good will of God for our lives. We have spent a limited amount of time walking in the presence of Jesus and haven't yet matured enough to be ready for the harvest. Then there are the tomatoes that have just started to turn light orange. This is the acceptable will of God for our lives. We have increased our time spent walking with Jesus, talking and listening to Him. As a light orange tomato, we could be picked for the harvest but would need to spend time on the shelf to finish ripening. Then Jesus showed me the fully ripe tomatoes ready for picking. These tomato skins have turned red from spending time in the presence of the sun, being nourished on the vine, coming to full maturity. By waiting until the tomato is fully ripe, you get a firm fruit with better flavor. When you are in the perfect will of God, you are walking in the maturity to know without a doubt what He is saying for you to do, you have proved the will of God for your life. Paul wrote to the church at Colossae this prayer.

> Colossians 1:9-10(KJV) – For this cause we also, since the day we heard it, do not cease to pray for you, and to desire that ye might be filled with the knowledge of His will in all wisdom and spiritual understanding; that ye might walk worthy of the Lord unto all pleasing, being fruitful in every good work, and increasing in the knowledge of God;

We should strive to walk in the will of God in every area of our life. Each daily decision should be taken to Him for direction. Our prayers should be that we be filled with the spiritual understanding, comprehension and awareness with insight into His purposes from being close to Him. Don't presume on the grace of God to keep you if you ignore walking in His will for your life.

> I Samuel 15:22(KJV) – And Samuel saith, Hath the Lord as great delight in burnt offerings and sacrifices, as in obeying the voice of the Lord? Behold, to obey is better than sacrifice, and to hearken than the fat of rams.

Our obedience to obeying the will of God for our lives is better than giving away all that we have. Discerning the will of God is only done by proving it, by walking in His presence, talking and listening to Him, sharing with Him the thoughts of your heart, and being able to understand more and more about Him. Are you a green tomato or can you prove you are a ripe tomato ready for the harvest by walking in God's perfect will for your life?

We give Him all praise and all glory.

14

Talk

Talk – to speak in order to give information or express ideas or feelings; converse or communicate by spoken words

In our progressive walk with Jesus, our relationship with Him takes us through several levels. And in doing so, our prayer life goes through changes also. The beginning of our walk is as a convert, meaning someone who has turned around in their way of thinking. Our first communication with Jesus is a prayer of repentance and a confession of faith, which begins to build our belief in Him. Then, as we go further down our path with Jesus, our prayers transform us to bring us closer to the image of Him.

> II Corinthians 3:18(KJV) – But we all, with open face beholding as in a glass the glory of the Lord, are changed into the same image from glory to glory, even as by the Spirit of the Lord.

Paul was telling the church at Corinth our hearts are changed by the Spirit of the Lord, a promise under the new covenant. Under the old covenant, the face of Moses was veiled so the children of Israel would not stare at the glory of God. Under this new covenant, our faces are unveiled and we reflect the glory of the Lord as if we are mirrors. Our countenance is being transformed by being progressively changed into His image from one degree of glory to even more glory by the Spirit of the Lord. It should be our desire to follow Him through this change, to allow the Holy Spirit to inhabit us and bring forth the gradual metamorphosis into a new creation. The old has passed away. In each step, we taste His goodness and witness the manifestation of His promises in our lives. At first, our prayers are generally for a need in our lives, self-seeking requests for personal areas. Then as you begin to see answers in prayers for yourself, you can feel more confident in praying for others with a more selfless outlook. Along the way, you begin to develop a closer relationship with Jesus, someone you can relate to on a more personal level.

> John 15:-13-14(KJV) - Greater love hath no man than this, that a man lay down his life for his friends. Ye are my friends, if ye do whatsoever I command you.

This scripture tells us the greatest show of love is when we lay down our lives for those around us. Don't think about this as actually perishing and breathing your last breath. To develop a close friendship, it must be cultivated and parts of your life must be sacrificed, allowing time for the other person. You must be found dependable, practice compassion for the other person, but most of all be in constant communication. How can you know what is going on with the other person unless you talk and share your heart? I can imagine Adam and Eve had this type of connection with God before they fell from the garden. Genesis 3:8 tells us that God was walking in the garden, calling out for them. Scripture doesn't tell us, but I would imagine that Adam had spent a lot of quality time talking to God. He wasn't a baby when he was placed in the garden. He had no schooling so how did he learn to speak? God fashioned a full-grown man out of the dust of the earth.

Was their communication on a more spiritual level? There were no other humans competing with him for an intimate closeness with his Creator. Adam had God all to himself. There were instructions from God on the care of the garden and the animals and with these duties, Adam had to be educated. So, I am sure Adam had quality time with his maker but he allowed a diversion to come between them. Sin initiated the digression of the relationship, which caused the interaction between God and Adam to be changed.

Today, too many Christians feel they are lacking in how to pray and talk to Jesus. They feel like they don't have the right words to speak. Part of our relationship with Jesus is based on His desire to be closer to us. His longing for us to open up our hearts to Him, spending quality time together that allows bonding and intimate interaction. What a friend we have in Jesus, none more thankful, none more true. Tell Him about your day. Unload the worries in your heart to Him, speaking them out loud. There is no better time to start than now. There is not a wrong way to do it. It doesn't have to sound verbose and poetic, just tell Him what's on your heart. Without developing this communication by not talking to Jesus, the relationship will fade. Can you lay down your life, turn off all that is going on within you, and focus on your relationship with Jesus, spending quiet time with Him? What do you talk to your friends about in the natural? You tell them what you have done today. The plans you might have for tomorrow. Conversations you have had with others and what is going on in their lives. Questions you have about something that has come up in your life. When you have started talking to Jesus, then truly listen to His responses, this is not a one-way conversation. This is a conversation with your most intimate friend, just between you and Him. It can start small, just a few minutes each day talking with Jesus, telling Him how things are going in your life, and then growing from glory to glory.

Ephesians 4:15(KJV) – But speaking the truth in love, may (we) grow up in Him in all things, which is the head, even Christ.

We give Him all praise and all glory.

15

Power

Power -the ability to do something or act in a particular way; move or travel with great speed or force.

How many of you are a fan of the Olympics? It takes dedication, determination, and power to accomplish the strength and stamina of these athletes to compete. The competitors train at an early age to build their bodies to take part in their chosen sport. For some, it is an increase in agility, and for some, it may be speed. However, this strength and stamina didn't come to these athletes overnight. There were endless hours spent exercising, running, and conditioning their bodies for just a few minutes of competition at the Olympics. Many compete for the metals that can be won at these games, but few win the gold, silver, or bronze rewards for a race well run. We, as sons of God, are being conditioned for such a race. Paul wrote in

> I Corinthians 9:24(KJV) – Know ye not that they which run in a race run all, but one receiveth the prize? So run, that ye may obtain.

Paul was telling the church at Corinth that all the runners run doing their very best, but only one receives the prize. He goes on to tell them that athletes must show a strong form of behavior and use self-control in everything to train and compete in the games. They do all of this training to receive a corruptible crown, but we train for an incorruptible crown. Each of us is placed in the body of Christ with a certain calling, a definite race or course that is God's will for our life. Our single-mindedness in how we spend our time, study the Bible, and get on our knees before the Father in prayer, should all be exercises in increasing our strength and power in the Holy Spirit. It is God's power in us that we need, to finish our race and live out the purposes of God in our lives.

> Ephesians 3:20(KJV) – Now unto Him that is able to do exceeding abundantly above all that we ask or think, according to the power that worketh in us.

Upon reading this scripture, we tend to focus on the 'abundantly above all that we ask or think', assuming it is just to be given by God. But the end of the scripture says it is done according to His power that works in us. That word power is the Greek word "dunamis" which means miraculous power, His power in us, not of ourselves. We see His keeping power in our lives, which is a witness to those around us, that miraculous power that heals, protects, provides, and loves unconditionally. And that same miraculous power works in us and through us to minister to others. But just as the athletes going to the Olympics, the miraculous power in us doesn't just show up. It must be cultivated, developed, built up, and imparted to us when the Holy Spirit falls upon us, as Jesus told the disciples.

Acts 1:7-8(KJV) - And He said unto them, It is not for you to know the times or the seasons, which the Father hath put in His own power. But ye shall receive power, after that the Holy Ghost is come upon you: and ye shall be witnesses unto Me both in Jerusalem, and in all Judea, and in Samaria, and unto the uttermost part of the earth.

In the first verse of these two scriptures, Jesus describes the power of the Father to know the times and seasons as the Greek word "exousia" which means a sign of regal authority. Because God is God, He alone has that ability and power to know the times and seasons, and it is not given to anyone else, not even Jesus. In the second verse, Jesus uses the Greek word "dunamis" for the power that is given to us after the Holy Ghost has come upon us to testify of Jesus. It is in walking with Him daily that this power increases. We start out as babes in the power of the Holy Spirit. But the more we wait on the Lord, allowing us to grow in His faith, being strengthened by His word, witnessing the goodness of the Lord, and walking out what He has for us, we begin to grow in the power of the Holy Spirit. Then, when you are filled with the Holy Ghost with evidence by speaking in tongues, your power from God gets even stronger. Just as with the Olympic athletes, our maximum power doesn't come overnight. The longer you train and practice, the more capable you become in His power. There is power in waiting on the Lord. You get stronger while you wait. And we are protected by that power.

II Peter 1:2-4(KJV) - Grace and peace be multiplied unto you through the knowledge of God, and of Jesus our Lord, According as His divine power hath given unto us all things that pertain unto life and godliness, through the knowledge of Him that hath called us to glory and virtue: Whereby are given unto us exceeding great and precious promises: that by these ye might be partakers of the divine nature, having escaped the corruption that is in the world through lust.

Peter is telling us that God has granted us His power, revealed to us true knowledge, and spoken to us with great promises. He is giving us everything necessary to live a dynamic spiritual life and godliness, through true and personal knowledge of Him who called us by His grace. But we need to be found faithful in what He has given us. We need to develop His power in our lives to walk in the witnessing He has for us in the coming days.

II Timothy 3:1-5(KJV) - This know also, that in the last days perilous times shall come. For men shall be lovers of their own selves, covetous, boasters, proud, blasphemers, disobedient to parents, unthankful, unholy, without natural affection, trucebreakers, false accusers, incontinent, fierce, despisers of those that are good, traitors, heady, high minded, lovers of pleasures more than lovers of God; having a form of godliness, but denying the power thereof; from such turn away.

Paul was writing to Timothy to be prepared. Hard times are coming, because pretentious, hostile, hateful, and betraying people are out there, even in the church. He tells Timothy to stay away from them. They may sound like they know God, they don't. Even though they look godly, they have denied the power (dunamis) of God that is available to us. It is that power that is the saving grace for us who walk with Him. It keeps us on the straight and narrow path that is Jesus Christ.

II Corinthians 4:7(KJV) – But we have this treasure in earthen vessels, that the excellency of the power may be of God, and not of us.

We must remember we are only containers, cracked pots, holding the divine strength of this power so that others may see it coming from God and not from us. All power belongs to the Lord to be used in these vessels of human frailty. We should purpose each day to grow in the power that He has given us to be steward over. There will come a time when you will be called forth to run the race. Will you be prepared in strength and stamina from walking in His power to make it to the finish line and win the prize?

We give Him all praise and all glory.

16

Standard

Standard – *a thing used as a measure or model in comparative evaluations, something set as a rule for measuring.*

A few years ago, my dad passed away at the age of 88. Just before he passed, he spent a short time in the hospital. But when he wouldn't agree to all the poking, prodding, treatments and testing they wanted to do on him, the hospital sent him home to be in the care of a hospice service. My parents have been very active in a denominational church for almost seventy years, including a church builders' program. During the hospital stay, many of the members of my parents' church came to visit my dad. And each time, my dad would ask them to pray and everyone would stand and pray at the bed. The first gentleman was someone who had spent time with my dad on several of the projects and committees and knew him quite well. When he was asked to pray, he said – Jesus, this is my friend, BJ. Take care of him, Jesus. And there wasn't a dry eye in the house. At the time, Jesus spoke to me and said – That is how I felt about my friend, Lazarus, when he had died. Then Jesus began to reveal all the things this man, my dad, lying in the hospital bed, had done in his lifetime. He was just my dad. He was just somebody I looked up to, but he was just my dad. There was correction in my life from him, but he was a standard. He stood on godly principles. He was married to my mom for sixty-six years. He retired from the company he worked for from the age of twenty-two, putting in almost 50 years of service. He was in the church all of my life, taking us to services every week, most times Sunday and Wednesday. Every week he read the bible to us and prayed with us. He was a standard for each of his children. Then Jesus spoke to me saying – "This is what I expect of You. I expect this standard every week, every day, every hour and every minute of your walk with Me. You are to be that standard, that rule for measuring in My Body".

Part of being a standard is mentoring; to be someone who advises and teaches. Do you realize what it takes to mentor someone? You can't mentor somebody you meet once. You can't mentor somebody you never see. You can't even mentor somebody over the phone. Your mentoring has to be one on one, every day, all day; speaking the word, being that standard. You need to be somebody who can teach them what they need to know. You must be someone who has spent their time with Jesus, in His word and in prayer; learning the things Jesus has taught you because only in that learning can you teach someone else. You can't teach what you haven't walked. We are to be a witness, someone who has seen and heard Jesus in our life. You can't be that witness if you haven't spent time in His presence and haven't heard His voice. You can't be that witness if the things He has done in your life can't be seen in you; if His keeping power cannot be seen in and through you. He will use you in a time when someone needs comfort, love, peace, and joy imparted into their life. We must be someone who can speak a word in season to those around us. And in that, you can be the witness He is looking for you to be.

As a standard, we need to be an encourager. We need to speak a reassuring word into the lives of those whom Jesus puts before us.

Have you told somebody how good they did or I love you this week and really meant it? All it takes is just a few words from a friend to make my day. A single word from you could brighten someone else's day and bring joy into their life. Those who don't have the Spirit of God in their life are bombarded by the words of the enemy continuously. And by the prompting of the Holy Spirit in your life, you can speak against that enemy, giving them just a little hope.

In order to be a standard for Jesus in the body of Christ, you must be found faithful. In everything Jesus gives you to do, be reliable, devoted, trustworthy, and dependable. It may not manifest in too many ways and is not an instant process. But with time, faithfulness can be seen in your life. You can't be a faithful servant without standing steadfast where Jesus has planted you until His appointed time. If you flit from place to place, not staying somewhere long enough to develop a spirit of faithfulness, how can you be found faithful in anything Jesus has called you to do?

There is a pattern that is set forth in a standard's life. How can people see Jesus if they don't see the pattern of Jesus in each of us? How can they see Jesus if they don't see what He has done in our lives and how we have changed and grown? There is a pattern there that can be done in their own life. They should desire the godly character that is observed in you to be manifest in their lives. The pattern is someone to come alongside and help them up.

> Galatians 6:1-9(KJV)– Brethren, if a man be overtaken in a fault, ye which are spiritual, restore such an one in the spirit of meekness: considering thyself, lest thou also be tempted.

In these scriptures, Paul was telling the church in Galatia, watch when your spiritual family has fallen into a trap and is snared by sin. Don't stand idle, but gently restore them, being careful not to step into your own snare.

> Vs 2(KJV) - Bear ye one another's burdens, and so fulfil the law of Christ.

Shoulder each other's burdens, come alongside, and offer encouragement, comfort, and peace.

> Vs 3(KJV) - For if a man think himself something, when he is nothing, he deceiveth himself.

But don't think that since you are a standard, you are above falling into the same snare.

> Vs 5(KJV) - For every man shall bear his own burden.

For you will have to bear your own burdens of faults and shortcomings, for which you alone are responsible.

> Vs 8-9(KJV) – For he that soweth to his flesh shall of the flesh reap corruption; but he that soweth to the Spirit shall of the Spirit reap life everlasting. And let us not be weary in well doing: for in due season we shall reap, if we faint not.

If you keep up the standard in your life, planting into other's lives, you shall of the Spirit reap life everlasting.

We are here to glorify Jesus in everything we do. But there is so much more that we are here for. There are so many that can't see Jesus yet. There are so many who don't know Him yet and don't walk in the fullness of Him. We are here to be salt and light, to be that encourager, that witness, that mentor, that pattern.

My dad was the first standard Jesus placed in my life. He was a mentor, a witness, an encourager, a faithful servant, and a pattern. We are a standard in other's lives. We are to be someone who comes alongside, to help others, to dig down into the source He has given us, and to give to others. But it will be in Jesus' time when it is done and in His way. He is building into each of us the foundation needed for His purpose. If a compromise comes into your life, your foundation rots. And as a pillar in the body of Christ, you fall. So, you have to keep the standard of what He is in your life to ward off compromise. Jesus is using each and every one of us to be a measure of His body to line up with. There will be times when you walk as a standard before the Lord and He will ask you to do something that you are uncomfortable doing. But we have to be stretched beyond to find out where His boundaries are in our lives. This stretching causes growth in His faith in us.

In the last five years, Jesus has planted new relationships in my life, as well as resurrecting and nourishing old ones. I am led to cultivate and develop these friendships on a regular basis. Taking time to meet each person, share what Jesus is doing in our lives, and offer encouragement and biblical words. I have learned that even though I am a standard in the relationship, Jesus may use my friend to speak a word into my life. It is a humbling experience to receive that word given by those who are learning to hear from Jesus. None of us has obtained the mark for the prize of the high calling of God in Christ Jesus. We are on a continual journey. Our goal should be the standard Jesus can use as a measure of rule before those who are looking for Him, that they might see Jesus in us.

We give Him all praise and all glory.

17

Coincidence

Coincidence - *a situation in which things happen at the*
same time without planning.

This week I went to the grocery store to pick up a few items. I stopped at the deli counter to get some cheese and a very personable lady waited on me. She asked how I was and I returned the same greeting to her. She answered that she was not doing good, as her father had just passed away. At the end of the transaction, I knew I couldn't just leave without ministering to her. But I wasn't quite sure how that was going to happen as the large deli counter was between us. I was led by the Holy Spirit to ask if I could give her a hug. She hesitated, but one of the other ladies behind the counter nodded Yes enthusiastically. So, I told the young lady to come down to the entrance to the deli, and I wrapped by my arms around her. In doing so, that put me in the perfect position to pray in her ear and allow Jesus to minister to her, filling her with His peace.

Was that a coincidence? As my steps are ordered by the Lord, I think not. That was the perfect timing of my Father in both of our lives. It was a step of faith for both of us, she to accept a hug from a stranger and me to move out and allow Jesus to use me. Most people these days are under the belief that their life is a sequence of coincidences, fate, or luck. Their walk is just situations that happen and they believe there is no higher power (whether good or bad) directing their steps. It is their idea that many areas of their life, including the job they have, their spouse, and their station in society, came about by chance or coincidence. That their life is what they make of it, allowing circumstances, conditions, and events to establish it. Because it is up to them to make their life what they want. But when you walk with God, your life is not your own.

> I Corinthians 6:19(KJV) – What? Know ye not that your body is the temple of the Holy Ghost which is in you, which ye have of God, and ye are not your own?

When you are God's, you have been bought with a price, purchased by the precious blood of Jesus, and you are to use your body to bring glory to Him. To walk in His will for your life, you allow Him to take control and work in your life as He sees fit; no matter where that takes you. You become the vessel for the Holy Spirit to dwell in and use to fulfill His purpose.

> Psalms 37:23(KJV) – The steps of a good man are ordered by the Lord: and He delighteth in his ways.

Those who are faithful and dedicated to walking in step with God are well pleasing unto God. There are no coincidences, no fate or luck; just the perfect timing of the Lord. When you are walking in step with Him, there is no room for anything but His perfect will for your life. Which could be your saving grace. He has ordered every step; He is the author and finisher of our faith. This could be waiting a few extra minutes before heading to work to answer that phone call you took from a friend who needed prayer. Maybe it is the car not starting that keeps you from going out when a disaster would have been in your path. It is those tiny miracles that maybe we don't realize when it happens, but because you are walking in the steps of Jesus, you are kept safe. Those steps could also put you in the presence of the girl behind the deli counter who had a broken heart because her father had passed. We never know where our path with Jesus will take us.

However, we do have the option to walk on this path or to choose another path of our own; a path of blessing or a path of cursing.

> Deuteronomy 30:19(KJV) – I call heaven and earth to record this day against you, that I have set before you life and death, blessing and cursing: therefore choose life, that both thou and thy seed may live:

Our life is a series of choices. Certain choices take us on the path of life and blessings, and other choices take us on the path of death and cursing. We are admonished to choose the path of life, which is Jesus Christ in our life with the indwelling of the Holy Spirit. Don't rely on coincidences to direct your life and make your decisions; resulting in the outcome of bad choices. As for me and my house, I serve a much greater power who orchestrates my life. And I thank Jesus every day that He is ever present in my life. I encourage you to keep your heart open to the prompting of the Holy Spirit in every step you take. You never know when just your loving touch and prayer will make a difference in a life; because in Jesus there are no coincidences.

We give Him all praise and all glory.

18

Integrity

Integrity – *the quality of being morally upright in spirit*

James 5:12(KJV) – But above all things, my brethren, swear not, neither by heaven, neither by the earth, neither by any other oath: but let your yea be yea; and your nay, nay; lest ye fall into condemnation.

In James' letter to the twelve tribes scattered abroad, he was reminding them of Jesus' instructions to let your yes be yes and let your no be no (a firm yes or no). The oath spoken of in this scripture is a promise to do or not do something, using God as a witness and Him to bring judgment if the oath is broken. Maybe to keep the oath, it could be sworn by something lesser, such as heaven or earth; allowing some flexibility in the breaking of the oath. Jesus says to simply say yes or no and mean it. Your oath should be your guarantee, sticking by what you say. Walk with integrity and uprightness in your heart.

Those of us who are called to be the children of God are called to walk in this higher standard. The Holy Spirit itself bears witness to our spirit and we are called to walk in uprightness before Him. As we are one of

His children, we are to reflect His righteousness for all the world to see, which includes loving our neighbor as ourselves.

In the New Testament, a certain lawyer approached and asked Jesus how he could inherit eternal life. Jesus asked him what is written in the law. The lawyer responded, Thou shalt love the Lord thy God with all thy heart, and with all thy soul, and with all thy strength, and with all thy mind; and love thy neighbor as thyself. Jesus agreed with him and told him to do those things and he would live.

> Luke 10:29-30(KJV) – But he, willing to justify himself, said unto Jesus, And who is my neighbor? And Jesus answering said, A certain man went down from Jerusalem to Jericho, and fell among thieves, which stripped him of his raiment, and wounded him and departed, leaving him half dead.

Jesus goes on in the parable to tell how a priest walked by the injured man, saw him and passed by on the other side. Now a priest is someone who is called to minister in the Temple; which includes twice a year performing the daily Temple sacrifices for a week. Much of the rest of his time was spent living at home, with a few priestly functions to perform; but otherwise working in an occupation. The second person to walk past the injured man was a Levite, who saw him and passed by on the other side. This man was also a priest in the temple, but of a distinct class, connected to the temple in Jerusalem, along with the priests. Both men were taught in the law of Moses and knew the commandments including Love thy neighbor as thyself. But neither of them stopped to help the injured man, knowing what was right in the sight of God, but choosing to keep walking. Having hard hearts, the priest and the Levite walked on by; unaffected by the condition of the wounded and battered man. But Jesus wasn't through with His parable. Along comes a man from Samaria, who was aware of what was going on around him. He saw the man lying beside the road with the eyes of his heart and felt compassion on him. Jesus doesn't tell us the heritage of the man who is lying beaten and battered, which tells us it doesn't matter, because everyone is precious in His sight. This parable was told to a lawyer who was an expert and teacher in Mosaic law; who would know the difference between a Jewish priest and a Samaritan man? Samaria had been at odds with Israel for several hundred years, and the hatred was on both sides. Citizens of Judea had spent centuries walling Samaritans out of their society with laws and mistreatment. But Jesus is saying a thousand years of disputes and arguing is enough, and it is time to take down the walls of division. To look at the three men, one would think that it would be the priest and Levite who had the most integrity. But they were so wrapped up in the legalism of the law that there was no compassion or love in their heart.

Proverbs 11:3(KJV) – The integrity of the upright shall guide them: but the perverseness of transgressors shall destroy them.

Not only are we to walk with integrity concerning the things of God, but we should strive for this same integrity in every area of our lives. As children of God, our witness should go forth in everything we do and say to those around us. Sometimes it seems that the crooked, dishonest person gets away with perverse behavior and prospers from it; from our politicians to businessmen. Deceit in any form causes people to suffer. If we don't start walking with integrity in our lives, we will see all around us destroyed as a result of the evildoers. Our yes or no should be without question to God for each purpose He sends us on. We should be a man of our word.

Proverbs 11:1(KJV) – A false balance is abomination to the
Lord; but a just weight is his delight.

During the time of the Old Testament, bartering was a means to
exchange goods. This was done with weights and balances on a scale.
The writer of Proverbs is referencing the use of deceptive weights in
their scales. The Lord hates cheating and delights in honesty. We are
to be guided by our desire to walk upright before the Lord with no need
to change. We are called to be blameless and innocent, to bring light
to a dark, crooked, and twisted generation. Let your yes be yes and
your no be no; never allow evil to set you on the fence.

We give Him all praise and all glory.

19

Self-control

Self-control – the ability to control oneself, in particular one's emotions and desires or the expression of them in one's behavior, especially in difficult situations.

There are parts of each of us we would so like to get under control. These are habits we have developed over the years that have taken a strong hold on us. As we grow older, we realize that they have caused a weakness and dependency on something that we find is not of God for our lives. When I got married, my husband smoked cigarettes. He had started smoking at an early age and had been smoking for about ten years by then. Over the years, he tried several different ways to curb his reliance on tobacco, trying everything from cigars to snuff, but could find no way to stop the craving. These desires for nicotine come from the brain. The receptors respond to your previous nicotine use and will increase the desire to smoke. That makes it very difficult to quit on your own power. When we had been married for about twelve years, we both were filled with the Holy Ghost by the evidence of speaking in tongues as the Spirit of God gives utterance. At that time, Phil's desire to quit smoking became greater and he prayed that Jesus would deliver him from this nicotine habit. The desire for the nicotine was immediately removed, and Phil did not smoke another cigarette for the rest of his life. After almost 25 years of the nicotine receptors in Phil's brain telling him he needed a cigarette, Jesus renewed his mind and delivered him from smoking. When we allow Jesus to take control of our weaknesses and give us His strength, then miracles can be done in our lives.

Habits, whether they be ones that attack our natural body or those that affect our emotions, can get out of control and begin to manipulate us. If you are telling me you have nothing that tries to control your life but Jesus, well try to do without sweets or bakery goods or any item that you enjoy eating. By your own self- control fast from eating that item and see how successful you are. If Jesus calls you on the fast, you are able to accomplish it through His strength. But doing it of your own will, under your self-control, you will find it very difficult and will often fail. Cravings for certain foods are not the only habit that we need to allow Jesus to deal with. Anything we find in our lives that we can't seem to let go of needs to be taken to Jesus, so He may help us overcome it. Paul wrote to the church in Corinth:

> I Corinthians 3:1-3(KJV) – And I, brethren, could not speak unto you as unto spiritual, but as unto carnal, even as unto babes in Christ. I have fed you with milk, and not with meat: for hitherto ye were not able to bear it, neither yet now are ye able. For ye are yet carnal: for whereas there is among you envying, and strife, and divisions, are ye not carnal, and walk as men?

Paul is saying that he was not able to address this group as people who walk by the Spirit; he had to speak to them as people who tend to think in merely human terms. And the reason why – they were still living in the flesh, not in the Spirit. The way to tell this is they were still fighting with one another, comparing themselves to others, and consumed with jealousy. They were no different than those who lived in the world and followed the carnal mind, dominated by human nature. As long as we grab for what makes us feel good or makes us look important, are we really different from the carnal man? The carnal mind tries to lead you instead of the Spirit. If you take it upon yourself to do something, you are trying to do it in your carnal mind. Are there parts of your life that you are still living in the flesh? When you are finally able, by the Spirit of God, to turn it over to Jesus, only then will you see results in your life.

> Romans 8:5-7(KJV) – For they that are after the flesh do mind the things of the flesh; but they that are after the Spirit the things of the Spirit. For to be carnally minded is death; but to be spiritually minded is life and peace. Because the carnal mind is enmity against God: for it is not subject to the law of God, neither indeed can be.

Those of us who think we can change ourselves by our own flesh, with our own self-control, are walking in a carnal mind. A mind focused on the flesh is declaring war against God; it defiles the authority of God's law and is incapable of following His path. For those who are living by the Spirit set their minds on His will and purpose.

> Galatians 5:16(KJV) – This I say then, Walk in the spirit, and ye shall not fulfil the lust of the flesh.

If we will walk in the Spirit, let the Spirit bring order into our life, and be responsive to His guidance, we will never give in to our selfish and sinful cravings. When you walk in the Spirit, you have lost all control of your life and are walking in the will of the Father for your life. When you have been transformed by the renewing of your mind, you will relinquish all self-control in your life. Walking in the flesh can be detrimental to us in the coming days. It is very important that we be sensitive to the Holy Spirit that resides in us to give us directions in the way we should go. By relinquishing all control to the Holy Spirit, you will walk in the good, acceptable, and perfect will of the Father, finding His peace everywhere you go.

We give Him all praise and all glory.

20

Hope

Hope – a feeling of expectation, confidence or trust

My hope is in Jesus, a confident expectation of what He has promised and its strength in His faithfulness. I don't know how anyone can live these days unless this is true in your life. Recent events have proven our hope can't be in government or even in man. It can't be in our job, our financial status, or even in those around us. Our hope can't be in anything of this world; it can only be in Jesus Christ and Him crucified. Putting your hope in anything of this world would be like standing on sinking sand. It will not hold you up. But we are built on a firm foundation, Jesus Christ. I will not trust the sweetest frame – meaning I will not trust in myself or any other person, but wholly in the name of Jesus. We have all been raised in a can-do generation where nothing is impossible if you just believe. If we continue in this mindset, we have taken our hope away from Jesus and put our confidence in ourselves. I know you are saying, But Philippians 4 says I can do all things through Christ who strengthens me. That word "do" doesn't mean to accomplish, but to be strong, to have the power to endure. We can do all things with the strength of God that we might complete His purposes in our lives.

My daily bible reading has been in the book of Job this month. Job 1:1(KJV) – There was a man in the land of Uz, whose name was Job; and that man was perfect and uptight, and one that feared God, and eschewed evil. Job was a man that was righteous and innocent. He was one who reverenced God and shunned evil. He was pious, rich, loyal, and a man who loved God. Among Easterners he was the most powerful and influential man. He had a large family, 7,000 sheep, 3,000 camels, 500 teams of oxen, 500 female donkeys, and a large number of servants. Job prayed over his family to purify them, much like we do, asking the Father to clean their hearts of any sins. We know the account of the conversation between God and satan concerning Job. God asked satan in Job 1:8(KJV), Hast thou considered my servant Job, that there is none like him in the earth, a perfect, and an upright man and one that feareth God, escheweth evil? Satan tells God – that is because You have made an hedge about him and his house. He then says, If you will take the hedge down from Your protection, destroy all that Job has and he will curse You to Your face. So satan was allowed to test Job. Three friends came to him to give him comfort, each having their own reasoning why God would do this to Job. The next 36 chapters in the book are three cycles of debate between Job and his three friends about why Job was going through all that had happened to him. Each friend had their own take for the reason of all that has happened to Job. Even Job's wife told him to curse God and die. By the end of the book, Job is blessed by God and his wealth is restored. In all Job went through, all the questions he had for God about why he was going through all of his afflictions, not once did Job curse God. Not once did Job say – Ok God, I give up. I don't believe you are there for me. I can do better for my life without You. Surely there is a better way than following God, putting all my hope in Him. No, Job believed God was there for him, even through his darkest time.

Every bitter pool, every tough obstacle in our lives, is an opportunity to keep our hope in Jesus. What did you learn from what you have been through this week? Did you come out on the other side and now are you able to help someone else make it through their troubles? The more that we abide in Him, the more that He can manifest His life through us. Are you manifesting the victory you have gained from going through the affliction, or did you lose your hope in Jesus?

> I Peter 3:14-15(KJV) – But and if ye suffer for righteousness' sake, happy are ye: and be not afraid of their terror, neither be troubled; but sanctify the Lord God in your hearts; and be ready always to give an answer to every man that asketh you a reason of the hope that is in you with meekness and fear;

Even if you suffer from doing what is right, you will receive a blessing. Don't let them frighten you and don't be intimidated. But in your heart, set Jesus apart as holy, acknowledging Him, giving Him first place in your life as Lord, recognizing He is your only hope. Then be able, when you are asked why you are not filled with worry, fear, or anxiety, to tell the reason for the hope that lives within you, giving thanks to God in Christ Jesus for all things.

> I Thessalonians 5:17-18(KJV) – Pray without ceasing. In everything give thanks; for this is the will of God in Christ Jesus concerning you.

How can you lose hope with the things that are going on around us right now, when we know that our hope is in Jesus? If we look at the things which are seen, our hope fades. We must keep our eyes on Jesus, for He is our only hope. When you turn on the faucet, you expect water. When you flip a light switch, you expect the electricity to light up the bulb. When you get a word from Jesus, do you expect it to come forth? Put your hope in Jesus and expect that He will perform His word.

We give Him all praise and all glory.

21

─────· ⚜ ·─────

Victory

Victory - *a success or triumph over an enemy in battle or war. ... the ultimate and decisive superiority in any battle or contest:*

> II Corinthians 10: 3-5(KJV) For though we walk in the flesh, we do not war after the flesh: (For the weapons of our warfare are not carnal, but mighty through God to the pulling down of strong holds;) Casting down imaginations, and every high thing that exalteth itself against the knowledge of God, and bringing into captivity every thought to the obedience of Christ;

We are definitely in a time of battle as we have never seen before in our lifetime. Darkness on the earth is just getting darker and light is getting brighter. Paul wrote to the church at Corinth that we do not fight according to this world's rules of warfare. The world doesn't fight fair, but we don't fight our battles the same way the world does – never have and never will. We don't use manipulation to achieve our goals. The weapons we have been given for spiritual warfare are powered by God to effectively pull apart the fortifications people hide behind. We serve a commander-in-chief that is all mighty, all powerful, all knowing. This battle is not in the physical, but in the imaginations, every high thing, warped philosophies, every thought that pits itself against the knowledge of the one true God. The enemy would like us to think that all is lost and our God is no longer in control. He whispers in our ear saying, "You might as well come over to my side, submit to the control I will have in this." The enemy would like to sow seeds of doubt and unbelief in our hearts. We need to just cast down those whispers and every high thing that puts itself above the knowledge of God and believe that the perfect will of God will be performed, no matter what the outcome of the circumstances around us. Let's look at how God handled a battle in the Old Testament.

Joshua brought the children of Israel out of Egypt across the Jordan river. He is told:

> Joshua 1:3(KJV) – Every place that the sole of your foot shall tread upon, that have I given unto you, as I said unto Moses.

Joshua and the children of Israel were able to cross over the Jordan three days later on dry ground. Several of the nations in Canaan heard how God was leading His people, doing miraculous works for them and the nations just folded. Everything was going great until they hit a wall at Jericho. Just as we do when we come to a wall in our walk with Jesus, Joshua began to look at Jericho's defense barricade; calculating how to best bring the wall down.

> Joshua 5:13(KJV) – And it came to pass, when Joshua was by Jericho, that he lifted up his eyes and looked, and behold, there stood a man over against him with his sword drawn in his hand: and Joshua went unto him, and said unto him, asked, Art thou for us, or for our adversaries?

He replied, "I am the Commander-in-Chief of the Lord's army." Joshua fell to the ground before him in reverence and worshiped him and said, "Give me your commands." The Commander told him, "Take off your shoes, for this is holy ground." And Joshua did. This act of submission shows us Joshua's understanding about who God is, but also about who God was to Joshua. By removing his shoes, Joshua is saying: This battle will be won in the spiritual not in the natural. Our military equipment, our strategy, our strength or endurance will be of no benefit. If this battle is going to be won, if there is to be victory, it will be won by God's power, His strength, and His Spirit!

God told Joshua that Jericho and its king and all its mighty warriors were already defeated, for God has given them to Joshua! Then He gave specific instructions about how to walk around the wall of the city of Jericho each day for six days. There was an order that needed to be followed, including the order of the participants of the march, how many times they were to march around the city, and that they were to be totally quiet during the marches. Then, on the seventh day, God's instructions were for them to walk around the city of Jericho seven times and the priests were to blow the trumpets. When they play a long final blast, then all the people are to give a mighty shout. The city walls would collapse in front of them and all the Israelites would charge in and take the city. Joshua and the children of Israel didn't have to raise a single weapon. There was no need for any strategy to plan. All they had to do was believe that God had gone before them and prepared a way for victory. Do you suppose the children of Israel wondered what the priests thought they were going to get accomplished by marching around the wall of Jericho? They had to believe that Joshua knew what he was doing. Joshua listened to the instructions of the Lord, he had taken off his shoes, showing his reverence and submission to Him, then he let God handle it. Who would have thought marching around a city and shouting would cause the walls to crumble? Nothing is too hard for the God we serve.

In the natural at this time, it is overwhelming, looking like our nation is about to be defeated. It looks like we are encompassed about on every side. But in II Kings 6, Elisha told his manservant when he saw all the horses and chariots of Aram's king, "Fear not, for they that be with us are more than they that be with them."

Our hope should be in the Lord, not in the outcome of what is happening in our nation's politics. We must have perspective on the goodness of God and the ability of God to keep us and our nation regardless of the circumstances. That is why the weapons of our warfare are not carnal. We can't wage this war in the natural. We should be spending this time in the presence of the Most High God, not watching what the media is reporting. The media will plant the imaginations, every high thing, warped philosophies, every thought that pits itself against the knowledge of the one true God in our minds if we let it. We don't know what the will of the Father is at this time, and we don't know how He is going to accomplish a victory. All we know is that He is faithful to take care of us. Joshua asked the Commander-in-Chief of the Lord's army to give him the commands, the instruction, the directions for how to take down the wall of Jericho. We should be on our knees before the Father, asking for what He would have us do at this time for His victory to come forth. We are going to see victory in this battle. We don't know what it will look like or how it will come. We just know that all we have to do is keep marching around the city and at the appointed time of the Father, the walls will crumble before us and there will be victory. Now, don't get your hopes up that your preconceived idea of what victory looks like will be the same that comes from the Father. Remember, He sees the whole picture and you only see what is right before you. Don't let doubt and unbelief fill your mind, instead stay in His Word, continue praying in tongues as the Spirit gives utterance, and watch to see what the goodness of the Lord in the land of the living will be.

We give Him all praise and all glory.

22

Depend

Depend – *be controlled or determined by. To rely on*

Our body depends on the air we breathe to stay alive, and to create energy to sustain itself and its activities. It is something that we do without thinking about, it is a natural reflex. But when that air supply is cut short, our body goes into panic mode and we are suddenly controlled by the fear of dying. We feel fear because we have come to depend on that air. Jesus wants us to learn how to lean and depend on Him; because it is Jesus in you that sustains you. He wants us to learn dependence on Him as a natural reflex, just like breathing. It is when we become confident in the power of who Jesus is that we walk in His ways.

> Proverbs 3:5-6 – Trust in the Lord with all thine heart; and lean not on thine own understanding. In all thy ways acknowledge Him and He shall direct thy paths.

Trust – be confident and sure. Lean – to support oneself. This scripture is telling us to place our trust in God, relying on Him completely; never depending on our own ideas and inventions. If we will give God credit for everything He does in our life, in turn He will smooth out our path.

It is difficult at times to turn your problems over to Jesus and instead follow the desire to lean on your own knowledge or understanding. We are more apt to try to figure out our solution and implement it ourselves. We think we know the better way or we don't want to wait on Jesus' timing. In Luke 15, Jesus spoke to the Pharisees and scribes the parable of the lost son, someone who thought he knew better for his life than depending on his father.

> Luke 15:11-13 – And He said, A certain man had two sons: And the younger of them said to his father, Father, give me the portion of goods that falleth to me. And he divided unto them his living. And not many days after the younger son gathered all together, and took his journey into a far country, and there wasted his substance with riotous living.

The father was the stabilizing force in his son's life. The son probably had everything he could want while living with his father and took for granted how fortunate he was. As the younger son, he probably felt the older son was getting more attention, more responsibility, and more freedom than he was. He was allowing discontent to seep into his thoughts, causing him to lean on his own understanding, thinking his father didn't have his best interest at heart. The more he dwelt on these thoughts, the more he decided he could do it better on his own, not having to depend on his father. He didn't try to talk his son out of it or keep him from leaving, knowing that tying the son down would only make him want to go his own way more. So, the father let him go, but I am sure the father's heart broke knowing it would be a hard lesson for the son. The son went to a far country, outside of any influence of his father. He then proceeded to squander his portion of the inheritance in a reckless and foolish manner. He spent everything he had on the whims of the heart, knowing he didn't have to account to anyone. He didn't apply the lessons he learned at his father's knee. He threw away and wasted all that he had. In the parable, Jesus says that a famine came to the land, and the son realizes that his father's servants have it better than him. He begins to see the error of his ways, understanding that his father knew what was best for him.

Aren't we just like the son in this parable? How many times have we been content sitting at Jesus' feet when another opportunity comes along and lures us away?   It looks good, sounds good, tastes good, but is it God? It is vital that we depend and rely on Jesus to keep us on the path He has for us, just as it is important to take our next breath. Sometimes, we veer off the path and go down a rabbit hole. We don't realize circumstances are so bad until there is a famine in the land and we have no food, no shelter. It is at this point that we should turn back to Jesus, knowing that when we depend on Him, He will supply all our needs according to His riches in glory. All we have to do is ask, and He is there.

Several years ago, my husband passed away. During our married life, he took care of all the financial affairs for us. Then after he was gone, I was alone to make all the decisions, and it was very daunting as I had depended on him so much. There didn't seem to be anyone in the natural I could turn to for advice. My natural family would have liked to take over my decision-making, but I knew that wasn't God for my life. I began to pray about what to do and Jesus gave me direction on each decision that had to be made. As all of my adult life I had depended on man in this area, it was easy to allow Jesus to take over. Now this is one area in my life where I have learned to depend solely on the leading of the Holy Spirit.

Psalms 115:11 - Ye that fear the Lord, trust in the Lord: He is their help and their shield.

Those who walk in humbleness before God, be confident that He has your best interest at heart and He will comfort, support, and protect you. It is very easy to become discontent with where Jesus has you right now, being impatient with how things are going. When you allow that discontent to fester, it causes you to lean to your own understanding about where you are in your life. The thoughts come in to convince you that you know a better way. Do you override what Jesus has said to you, the directions He has spoken in your life and go off to squander all the blessings He has placed in your life? We can't walk this journey on our own. We must depend on Jesus to lead us and guide us in the way we must go, to trust that He has our best interest at heart. We must learn to rely, trust, and depend on Him in every area of our lives.

We give Him all praise and all glory.

23

Timing

Timing – the choice, judgment, or control of when something should be done especially having a good or bad effect on the result.

Ecclesiastes 3:1-2 – To every thing there is a season, and a time to every purpose under the heaven: a time to be born, and a time to die; a time to plant, and a time to pluck up that which is planted:

Looking at the word "season", we know there are four divisions of the year(spring, summer, autumn, and winter) for particular weather patterns and daylight hours. We can count on these four seasons occurring every year without hesitancy. In this verse, the word season is referring to a fixed and definite time for an appointed occasion. The verses go on to explain that there is a season and a time for all things; an exact period for everything under heaven. When God created the heavens and the earth, He set into motion times and seasons for all natural things.

Genesis 1:14(KJV) – And God said, Let there be lights in the firmament of the heaven to divide the day from the night; and let them be for signs, and for seasons, and for days, and for years:

This was God's perfect plan for the earth, that the sun and the moon would form day and night as well as measure the seasons. In nature around us, it is easy to see the times and seasons. The leaves on the trees turn orange, yellow, and brown; it must be autumn. Tulips pop up out of the ground; it must be spring. The trees and the tulips have purpose under heaven and at the appointed time, they are faithful to fulfill it. In our walk with Jesus, sometimes, it is difficult to know the times and the seasons for our lives. But if we seek the Father, He is faithful to show us His perfect will for our lives, which includes the times and seasons.

Isaiah 55:10-11 – For as the rain cometh down, and the snow from heaven, and returneth not thither, but watereth the earth, and maketh it bring forth and bud, that it may give seed to the sower, and bread to the eater: so shall My word be that goeth forth out of My mouth: it shall not return unto me void, but it shall accomplish that which I please, and it shall prosper in the thing whereto I sent it.

Just as the rain waters the earth from heaven and brings forth the bud, so shall the word that God has declared for your life be accomplished and not fall to the earth void. All the words from God that have been spoken over your life shall come to pass, maybe not in our timing, but definitely in the Father's time. The words will do the work in your life and complete the assignment He gave them. It is our responsibility to take the words in faith that were spoken and wait on the perfect timing of the Father to complete them.

The spring garden I planted this year has come to its end, and I decided to try growing a fall garden. But at this time of year, it is difficult to find starter plants in the nursery of the vegetables I wanted to grow. So, I decided to grow my own seedlings from scratch. I purchased the packets of seeds and planted them in the prepared soil in starter pots. Then I started waiting. I have watered them faithfully every day. I made sure they were getting enough sunlight, but not too much sun. And then there is more waiting. I checked the back of the seed packets for average germination time and it is going to be ten days. So, I am still waiting and not a sign of any fruit or even a leaf. Working with these seeds is much like dealing with the timing of the Lord. He has planted a seed in your spirit, a word spoken by God. This scripture in Isaiah 55 referenced above, gives us the promise that His Word shall be that goes forth out of His mouth: it shall not return unto Him void, but it shall accomplish that which He pleases, and it shall prosper in the thing whereto He sent it. If God said it, He will perform it; but probably not in our time. Just like the seeds planted in the prepared soil with the hard outer shell that needs to be softened for the seedling to come forth, there are areas in us that need to be dealt with before it is the right timing for God's word to come forth in us. Which means there will be some waiting. What should we be doing while we are waiting for the timing of the Lord? We should be getting before Jesus to find out the purpose He has for our lives at this time. We need to be continually growing in the things of the Lord and as we grow, our purpose in Him increases as well. While we wait our strength is rising, our hope in Him is rising and His faith that dwells in us is rising. Every time we wait on Him, we get a little stronger.

> Isaiah 40:31 – But they that wait upon the Lord shall renew their strength; they shall mount up with wings as eagles; they shall run, and not be weary: and they shall walk, and not faint.

The waiting that renews strength is not a passive instruction in this scripture. There are three action words given to us to do while we wait. The first one is to mount up – you shall spread your wings and soar like eagles, to come up before God. The second one is to run – to move rapidly. And then to walk – to continue in a forward motion. While we are waiting, we should spend our time worshiping God for what He is going to do in our lives, not muttering about having to wait. We should soar up into the heavens in praise and worship to Him. Then, as He begins to show you the purpose He has for you at this time, you should move rapidly toward it and continue to walk out what He is doing in your life. If we try to hold on to the old purpose in our lives, we can miss out on His greater plan.

It is not our position to question the timing of the Lord. The God we serve never gets tired out or pauses to catch His breath. He created all things that you can see and things you can't see. He knows everything, inside and out. So why would we want to hold onto the old plan and not want to walk into the full purpose He has for our lives? God's timing is always perfect. God is never late, never early, but always on time. Our timing is not God's timing, which often feels like a long, desperate delay. But there are two benefits in waiting for God's timing, it increases your faith, as you are forced to wait and trust in God. Plus, it makes certain that He, and only He, gets the glory and praise for bringing us through. In our walk with God, our desire should be to wait on His perfect timing for every area of our lives. If we allow Jesus to order our steps, we will always be in His timing.

We give Him all praise and all glory.

24

Wineskin

Wineskin – an ancient container made of animal skin, usually from goats or sheep, used to store or transport wine.

In biblical time wine was put into new wineskins, because as it ferments, the wine generates carbon dioxide gas that exerts pressure on the skin bottles, which were flexible. The process of making these wineskins included finding skins from goats or sheep from selected farms. The skin was then oiled with a resin to keep it supple during the fermenting process of the wine. And as the wine was consumed out of the container, the skin would dry out; causing it to become brittle. Jesus used this illustration in a parable.

> Luke 5:37-38(KJV) – And no man putteth new wine into old bottles; else the new wine will burst the bottles, and be spilled, and the bottles shall perish. But new wine must be put into new bottles; and both are preserved.

The word used for 'new' in these scriptures doesn't apply to the age of the skin. They didn't throw the old skins away and make completely new, unused skins. The word translates to mean a freshness. The old used skins were oiled again to make them supple and flexible to contain the new wine as it ferments. They didn't get rid of the vessel, just rubbed and lubricated the skins to bring back the new essence. Just as the Holy Spirit does to us in the spiritual.

> II Corinthians 5:17(KJV)– Therefore if any man be in Christ, he is a new creature: old things are passed away; behold, all things are become new.

The word 'new' in this scripture is the same word used when Jesus spoke of the new wineskins. He doesn't throw us away because we have dried out, He fills us with the Holy Spirit and we become lubricated and supple, ready for the Master's use. We become new. But some choose to remain in the old wineskins with a carnal nature; not allowing the Spirit to make them new again. Why would we want to put new wine into an old wineskin? It is our carnal nature to go the easiest route. It is just simpler to keep the old wineskin for the Holy Spirit to fill; this way we don't have to make sacrifices. We want to hold on to the old while receiving the new. We can't have it both ways. But, just as in the natural, it is in the spiritual. We can't keep our old carnal nature and be filled with the indwelling of the Holy Spirit.

Several years ago, I sold my home of 2200 square feet and moved into my current home that I share with my sister. As my portion of the new home is only 700 square feet, I knew I had to downsize my belongings. Some items were an easy decision and purging them was no problem. However, there were a few items that were a little harder to let go of. Items that I had for a long time or those that held fond memories were the most difficult to release. I knew that if I took all the items from my old house into my new house, there wouldn't even be room to walk around. I also realized that taking care of a house that had 2200 square feet would have consumed my time and finances and moving into a smaller home just made sense in the natural. This is the same condition we have in the spiritual in our life. We have filled our lives with things in the spiritual and natural that take away our focus from Jesus. When Jesus calls us to walk with Him and to grow into Him in the spirit, all the carnal things in our lives have to be released. We must choose to let go of all the idols, obsessions, traditions, philosophies, and carnal nature that are holding us back. In doing so, there is not just more space; but also, freedom, liberty, and time made for all the new things Jesus is calling us into.

> Ephesians 4:22-24(KJV) – That ye put off concerning the former conversation the old man, which is corrupt according to the deceitful lusts; and be renewed in the spirit of your mind; and that ye put on the new man, which after God is created in righteousness and true holiness.

Take off your former way of life, and completely discard your former nature, which has been corrupted by devious desire and covetousness. Then let God take your wineskin and make it new again, by being renewed by the Holy Spirit that now dwells in you. The result of this is that you are created into a new man, walking in the likeness of God: truthful, righteous, and holy. The book of Acts tells us about the gathering of the disciples when the day of Pentecost was fully come. They were all gathered in one place. Suddenly there came the roar of a violent wind and the whole house reverberated with sound. A flame appears, dividing into smaller flames and spreading from one person to the next. All those present are filled with the Holy Spirit and begin speaking in tongues as the Spirit gives utterance. As it was a holy festival, there were Jews who heard the sound and could hear the group speaking in their native languages. They all wondered how this could be. Skeptics claimed they must be drunk on new wine. Peter stands up along with the other eleven and tells the crowd they are not drunk, as they suppose, seeing it is only nine o'clock in the morning. He tells the crowd this is the manifestation of what was spoken by the prophet Joel.

> Acts 2:17-18 – And it shall come to pass in the last days, saith God, I will pour out of my Spirit upon all flesh: and your sons and your daughters shall prophesy, and your young men shall see visions, and your old men shall dream dreams: and on my servants and on my handmaidens I will pour out in those days of my Spirit; and they shall prophesy:

God has poured out that same Spirit on those that are His; those that are filled with evidence of speaking in another tongue as the Spirit gives utterance. That filling is just the beginning of the new wine the Spirit is putting into your new empty wineskin. We have a choice – new wine in new wineskins or new wine in old wineskins. This choice is imperative to our existence. There is so much that our Father has for each of us – prophecy, visions, dreams, and more; but it can't exist along with the old fallen nature. The old man must be "put off" and the new man must be "put on". Romans tells us not to be conformed to this world, but to be transformed by the renewing of our mind. The choice is ours to choose; the old or the new. Life or death. Put off the old carnal nature and let the Holy Spirit move, renewing your wineskin to be supple and pliant for God to use. Allow Jesus to make your wineskin fresh and new, so He can fill it with all that He has for you. You can do this through the power of Jesus Christ, who loves you.

We give Him all praise and all glory.

25

Distraction

Distraction – *a thing that prevents someone from giving full attention to something else.*

Matthew gives us an account in the New Testament of an excellent case of distraction. Jesus had just heard of the death of John the Baptist and had departed into a desert place to be alone with the Father. When the people heard, they followed Him. Jesus was moved with compassion when He saw them and performed miracles, including feeding the five thousand men, beside women and children. When it was time to depart, He compelled His disciples to get into a ship and go to the other side while He sent the multitudes away. Jesus then went up into a mountain alone to pray. When it became evening, He was alone on the shore, but the ship was in the middle of the sea. The wind had picked up, and the ship was being tossed by waves. Jesus walked on the water to the ship and when the disciples saw a figure approaching them, they were afraid, thinking it might be a ghost. Jesus spoke, saying Be of good cheer; it is I; be not afraid.

> Matthew 14:28-30(KJV) – And Peter answered Him and said, Lord, if it be Thou, bid me come unto Thee on the water. And He said, Come. And when Peter was come down out of the

ship, he walked on the water, to go to Jesus. But when he saw the wind boisterous, he was afraid; and beginning to sink, he cried, saying, Lord, save me.

As long as Peter kept his eyes on Jesus, he could walk on the water. But the minute the distraction of the wind blowing hard, the waves lapping up his legs, and the removal of something solid under his feet, Peter took his eyes off of the Lord and focused on his circumstances. The whispers in Peter's ear told him that walking on the stormy water was not possible. What was he thinking believing that Jesus could just call him and he would be able to walk out to Jesus? When Peter's attention was on the Lord, he was walking in single-mindedness. But scripture tells us you cannot serve two masters. Your focus must be totally on what Jesus is asking you to do.

Proverbs 4:25-27(KJV) – Let thine eyes look right on, and let thine eyelids look straight before thee. Ponder the path of thy feet, and let all thy ways be established. Turn not to the right hand nor to the left: remove thy foot from evil.

In this proverb, we are admonished to keep our heads up, our eyes focused directly in front of us. Don't deviate off the path Jesus has you on, that path that leads to His perfect will for your life. So don't allow distractions to take your attention to the right or left, but look straight ahead. Sometimes this is difficult. Someone comes along that wants you to do something for them. What they are asking you to do is not something bad, but it is good. Usually, you are more than capable of doing the task asked of you, so that is not a logical opposition to doing the favor. But what about the time aspect. Did you figure in the time that would be taken away from focusing on God? Good distractions are a weapon of the enemy to get you off of your progressive trip to the perfect will of God for your life. The enemy will use distractions to keep us busy, causing us to be worn out and lose our focus. God wants us to focus on the pathway to the perfect will He has for our lives. Distractions are the most unrecognized weapon of the enemy to get Christians off track. The enemy of perfect is to allow the good will of the Father to take top priority.

> Romans 12:2(KJV) - And be not conformed to this world: but be ye transformed by the renewing of your mind, that ye may prove what is that good, and acceptable, and perfect, will of God.

Don't follow the crowd and allow them to mold you into their image. The crowd would have you fill your time with projects and activities. These will endeavor to use up not only your time, but all of your energy, causing you to have none left to spend with the Lord. We are called to be progressively changed by focusing our mind to be more Christlike. You do this by spending more time in His word, seeking His face in prayer, and listening for His voice spoken to you. In this transformation, you learn to hear the difference between the enemy's voice and Jesus' voice. By doing so, you can easily determine which is a distraction and which is the will of God; that you may demonstrate to yourself what is good, what is acceptable, and what is perfect for your life.

> I Corinthians 7:35(KJV) – And this I speak for your own profit; not that I may cast a snare upon you, but for that which is comely, and that ye may attend upon the Lord without distraction.

Paul is writing to the church at Corinth concerning decisions they are making regarding their lives. He was using the dynamic of the husband/wife relationship as opposed to the relationship of each person with Jesus. This word 'distraction' is a derivative of the word meaning to drag around, to be over-occupied. We will always be in relationships, but how you prioritize the people in your life is what is important. We will always have someone in our lives who tries to take first place and distract us from God. Jesus tells us the first and great commandment that we have been given is to love the Lord with all our heart, with all our soul, and with all our mind. That is with all of our passion, our understanding, and our living, breathing body. Anything that attempts to be placed above that love from us to Him should be set aside.

> Hebrews 12:1(KJV) – Wherefore seeing we also are compassed about with so great a cloud of witnesses, let us lay aside every weight, and the sin which doth so easily beset us, and let us run with patience the race that is set before us.

Take an inventory of your life. Are there items you need to set aside that are distracting you from your time with Jesus? You need to make a decision for a permanent change of attitude, laying down and pushing the distraction far away and beyond your reach. I have found in my prayer time, my time set aside to ponder on the goodness of God, that the enemy will use the distraction of the things in my room that need to be done, all the projects that need to be completed. I prayed for wisdom on how to lay aside that weight and was instructed to turn off the lights and close my eyes while I prayed. Now my focus is directly on Jesus and I have set aside one distraction, trying to keep me from my time of closeness with Him. Learn to listen to the voice of Jesus concerning directions for you instead of the enemy. Events of this time are trying to distract us. Don't be troubled by what is going on around you; don't listen to the distractions being whispered in your ear. Lift your head, keep your focus on what God is doing in your life.

We give Him all praise and all glory.

26

Boundary

Boundary – a dividing line, something that indicates or fixes a limit or extent.

We all have boundaries, lines, and limits in our lives; whether they are self-imposed or placed there by others. And when we cross these lines, we can cause damage. Whether it be by something inappropriate we said into someone's life or we physically moved out of our designated space, much like driving a car. You learn when you start driving that there are limits you need to be aware of, and that must be observed. First, we are given speed limits on how fast we can drive; which are imposed for two reasons: to help us safely maneuver the road and to keep us going in the flow of the traffic. Second, the road is divided into lanes. Staying in your lane keeps you from playing bumper cars with the others; which would cause traffic conflicts. New car models also have preset alarms for other boundary notifications, such as following too close or a car in your blind spot. Our walk with Jesus is much the same with boundaries and limits. Even Jesus asks permission to cross a boundary between you and Him.

Revelation 3:20(KJV) – Behold, I stand at the door, and knock: if any man hear My voice, and open the door, I will come in to him, and will sup with him, and he with Me.

Jesus is telling us He will stand still at the door of our hearts and wait for us to invite Him in. He doesn't barge in; He waits for us to open the door. Then He will come in. Isaiah 30 tells us the Lord will wait, that He may be gracious unto us. The Lord longs to be merciful to us and He waits until we acknowledge Him to have kindness toward us. Even Jesus acknowledged His boundaries and honored them. Paul wrote in Philippians 5 – Let this mind be in me which was also in Christ Jesus. Jesus submitted to the will of the Father and came to earth a man to die for our sins. He accepted the boundaries of human flesh, the measure of rule that was given to Him while He was walking on the earth. Paul was asking for this same mind of Christ in dealing with the measure of rule that was given to him. When Jesus places you in His church as He sees fit, then you have been given by God a measure of rule, a boundary that is your area.

II Corinthians 10:13(KJV) – But we will not boast of things without our measure, but according to the measure of the rule which God hath distributed to us, a measure to reach even unto you.

The Greek word for 'measure' is metron, which means a limited portion or share. Paul is writing to the church at Corinth concerning the measure they have in their lives. They had begun comparing themselves among themselves. Paul is saying they should not make themselves the measure of others, feeling that they are superior. We each have our own measure of rule, our own part of the body of Christ to minister to and take care of. If everyone did what they wanted in

108

the body, there would be chaos. In the carnal world, you compare yourself to others, which means measuring others on a human scale against where you have come in the Lord. When we let the Spirit measure us through God's Word, He measures us on God's ruler. He looks at the heart. Paul is saying we all should be running in our own lane and not in someone else's. We are each given a domain, a territory to have authority over. It is important that we not exercise authority outside that area. Don't presume by your own mind that what you have heard from God for your life is exactly what everyone else needs. Only step out by the prompting of the Holy Spirit.

In I Corinthians, Paul is writing to the church regarding the distinct gifts given to each member in the body of Christ. In the first part of the chapter, he lists out the fruit of the Spirit, but tells the church they work by one Spirit in each member separately.

I Corinthians 12:12, 14(KJV) – For as the body is one, and hath many members, and all the members of that one body, being many, are one body: so also is Christ. For the body is not one member, but many.

Paul goes on to describe how the physical body has many different parts, but it takes all these parts to keep the body functioning. The eye never decides it wants to be an ear and tries to start hearing. It's function is to see and report what it sees to the rest of the body. The parts of the body never cross boundaries into another part's domain. Much like the body of Christ, it takes many parts to make up our human body.

I Corinthians 12:17-18(KJV) – If the whole body were an eye, where were the hearing? If the whole were hearing, where were the smelling? But now hath God set the members every one of them in the body, as it hath pleased Him.

Just because you are a foot and not an eye, doesn't mean you are not an important part of the body. As a member of the body of Christ, we have been set in a specific place meant just for us. We have each been set in the body of Christ to fulfill His purpose in our lives. Jesus makes our measure of rule just the perfect size and shape to fit into the plan He has for the body of Christ. In my walk with Jesus, I have caught myself comparing my measure of rule to others around me. I felt like I was the little toe in the body of Christ and desired to have what others did. As Jesus began to make areas in my measure clear to me and opened them up, I saw my lines begin to move and increase. When we have been faithful with what He has given us, He can increase our boundaries, but not until we have been found to be a good steward of what we already have. Ask Jesus to show you the boundaries He has set in your life, so that He may use you to your fullest potential.

We give Him all praise and all glory.

27

Kindness

Kindness – the quality of being friendly, generous, and considerate

Ephesians 4:32(KJV) – And be ye kind one to another, tenderhearted, forgiving one another, even as God for Christ's sake hath forgiven you.

Paul has just instructed the church at Ephesus to let go of all their bitterness, anger, and evil speaking. He is saying you have a choice in your attitude, an option on how you react to others. You can choose to be bitter, harsh, and unforgiving when someone offends you. Or you can take the high road and be compassionate, kind, forgiving, just as God has forgiven you. Just consider how much God has pardoned and shown kindness to you over your lifetime; all the times you have messed up and turned to Him for forgiveness. Has He held back any forgiveness toward you? Should we not, with the degree of kindness God has shown us, show that same kindness to those around us?

I attended a New Year's conference at a local church recently. I have only been to this church a few times, and didn't know many people there. At one service, a lady came in to sit in the row where I sat with her arms full of various items. She was having a difficult time maneuvering all she had plus a walking cane, which was starting to tip over from its propped position. I reached over and put my hand on the cane to stabilize it and asked if it was in the position for when she needed it. She said it was and thanked me for my help. Several other connections were made with this woman during that church service. When I got up to leave, she thanked me for being so kind and said she looked forward to seeing me in the future. I saw a need and felt the prompting of the Holy Spirit to step in and help make someone's load a little lighter. Too many times, we are focused on ourselves and not on the things that are going on around us. It would have been easy to continue with my concentration on the services and let her struggle with her burden. But I chose to let the love of Jesus shine through me to someone who needed a little brightness in her life.

In Luke, Jesus told the parable of the man from Samaria as an example of how we are to respond to those in need. A certain man was traveling from Jerusalem to Jericho and was attacked by thieves, stripping him of his belongings, wounding him, and leaving him for dead. Now there were two men of God, a priest and a Levite who passed by the suffering man and just crossed the street to pass by on the other side. A priest was someone who was chosen among all the Levites to perform temple related ministering and functions as a religious leader. Whereas, a Levite occupies a lesser place than the priest does. His place in the temple comes from having a pedigree of being born in the Hebrew tribe of Levi. Both men had extensive education in the laws of Moses and followed them legalistically. Sometimes it is difficult to understand the implication of what we are being told in the scripture without some of the background. The Jewish and Samaritan religious leaders taught that it was wrong to have any interaction with a conflicting group, even though they were both taught to love your neighbor as yourself. I am sure the priest and the Levite thought they were above stopping to help out, but these are the two people who should have stopped without even thinking about it, as it was part of their calling. Then along came a Samaritan and helped the injured man by putting him in an inn for the night. Now Samaria and Judah had been warring for many years; a Jew would even walk the long way around to get from Jerusalem to Galilee, instead of taking the shorter, direct route through Samaria. Let's just say the Jews and the Samaritans did not like each other. The verses don't tell us what nationality the wounded man was, but to the Samaritan, it didn't matter. He saw a need and stepped in to help.

Jesus used this parable to teach a lesson to a lawyer well versed in Mosaic law. The man had asked Jesus, "What shall I do to inherit eternal life?" Jesus' reply to the question was another question in Luke 10:26(KJV) - What is written in the law? How readest thou? The answer he gave to those questions was:

Luke 10:27(KJV) – And he answering said, Thou shalt love the Lord thy God with all thy heart, and with all thy soul, and with all thy strength, and with all thy mind; and thy neighbour as thyself.

Jesus told him he answered correctly. But the lawyer wasn't quite satisfied with that answer. I am sure the lawyer would not have stopped to help the wounded man on the side of the road. He needed to justify certain unclean, unholy situations that would keep him from loving his neighbor as himself, his lack of love for some kinds of people. What keeps us from showing kindness to all those around us, those who don't walk the same faith walk that we do, those who rely on doctors and drugs for their healing, those who have a different outlook

113

on the way we should be governed? It is easy to show kindness and love to those who are just like us, but a stretch in our walk to even begin to accept those who are different, much less show them kindness.

Peter wrote in his letters to those who have received the precious faith through the righteousness of God and Jesus Christ:

> II Peter 1:2(KJV) – Grace and peace be multiplied unto you through the knowledge of God, and of Jesus our Lord.

If we want more and more of God's kindness and peace in our lives, then we must learn to be more like Him and to know Him better. It is His kindness toward us that we should use as an example of the kindness we show to others. A little kindness goes a long way in mending hurt feelings, and repairing the rift between two people, building a bridge in an otherwise broken relationship. But you must choose to take the first step; allow Jesus to shine through you with the love that will heal all. He has shown kindness to you. Can you risk showing kindness to others?

We give Him all praise and all glory.

28

Temple

Temple – A building devoted to the worship, or regarded as
the dwelling place of God.

> I Corinthians 3:16-17(KJV) – Know ye not that ye are the
> temple of God, and that the Spirit of God dwelleth in you? If
> any man defile the temple of God, him shall God destroy; for
> the temple of God is holy, which temple ye are.

In chapter 3 of I Corinthians, Paul was writing to the church at Corinth
admonishing them for their infantile actions with each other. He
described them as babes in Christ, because of the envy, strife, and
divisions. The church members were saying; I am of Paul; and another,
I am of Apollos; but Paul says that is a fleshly nature being manifested.
Paul goes on to describe how each of us is God's temple. Jesus Christ
laid the foundation in us; then sent the Holy Spirit to start the building
process of His temple. Paul tells us in this same chapter:

> I Corinthians 3:12(KJV) – Now if any man build upon this
> foundation gold, silver, precious stones, wood, hay, stubble;

Paul is telling us one day the building will be tested by fire. If it stands
the test, he will be rewarded. But if it is built of wood, hay and stubble,

it will be consumed by the fire. What materials are you putting in your temple of God?

The first temple of God in the earth was the tent that Moses built. It was built as a tent because the children of Israel wandered around the wilderness for 40 years, so the temple had to be mobile to go with them. It was built with specifications that God gave to Moses. In the second year after the children of Israel left Egypt, Moses began to erect the tent just as he had been instructed. He covered the frame of the tent with tent fabric and then covered that with other pieces they had made. After the tent was raised, Moses began to move all the fittings into place; including the ark of the covenant, the candlesticks, the table of shewbread, and the golden altar. When the work was finished, the presence of God filled the temple.

> Exodus 40:34-35(KJV) – Then a cloud covered the tent of the congregation, and the glory of the Lord filled the tabernacle. And Moses was not able to enter into the tent of the congregation, because the cloud abode thereon, and the glory of the Lord filled the tabernacle.

The children of Israel used the cloud that blanketed the tent to guide them through all of their wanderings in the wilderness by day and a pillar of fire to guide them by night. The tent was not only a pilot to guide them, but it was also a place of worship and to give offerings and sacrifices. For over three hundred years, this mobile temple served as a dwelling place for God to abide with His people. Then came King David, who adored God, highly respected His laws, and loved Him above everyone and everything in his own life. David's desire was to build a tabernacle for God, but God told him there was too much blood on his hands from war. But God promised that David's son, Solomon, would build the Tabernacle. Solomon began to build the temple in the fourth year of his reign. As best as I can, I will try to describe the opulence and grandeur of the tabernacle. It was 90 feet long and 30 feet wide with a porch of 30 feet, and the porch was covered in gold on the inside. The inside of the tabernacle was paneled with gold-covered cypress wood that was engraved with palm trees and ornamental chains. Then it was entirely decorated with precious stones. At the back of the Tabernacle was the Holy of Holies, an additional 30 square feet gilded in 23 tons of gold, which in today's market would be worth $1.5 billion dollars. The area where the presence of the Lord abides had the most gold. The Tabernacle, both the Holy Place and the Holy of Holies were filled with golden vessels to be used by the priests. When the tabernacle was completed, King Solomon called an assembly for a dedication service.

II Chronicles 5:11-14(KJV) – And it came to pass, when the priests were come out of the holy place: (for all the priests that were present were sanctified, and did not then wait by course: Also the Levites which were the singers, all of them of Asaph, of Heman, of Jeduthun, with their sons and their brethren, being arrayed in white linen, having cymbals and psalteries and harps, stood at the east end of the altar, and with them an hundred and twenty priests sounding with trumpets:) It came even to pass, as the trumpeters and singers were as one, to make one sound to be heard in praising and thanking the Lord; and when they lifted up their voice with the trumpets and cymbals and instruments of musick, and praised the Lord, saying, For He is good; for His mercy endureth for ever: that then the house was filled with a cloud, even the house of the Lord; So that the priests could not stand to minister by reason of the cloud: for the glory of the Lord had filled the house of God.

The musical praise coming from the priests and the musicians must have been awesome. Just the one hundred and twenty priests sounding their trumpets would have been an overwhelming sound. The voices of all the priests and the music of all the instruments came together in unison. The trumpets playing their part, the clashing of cymbals and the thunderous playing of the other musical instruments plus the vocal group singing as one, saying, For He is good, His mercy endureth forever; ushered in the presence of God. His presence completely filled the temple so that the priests could not stand to minister.

This is the degree of the presence of God in my life that I desire; all of Him and none of me is able to stand up. Jesus showed me that the presence of God was in the tent that Moses built moved to the Tabernacle Solomon built, and dwelled there until Jesus' death. Matthew 27 tells us that when Jesus gave up the ghost, the veil of the tabernacle was rent in two from the top to the bottom. The veil was the separation of the presence of God and mortal man, and there was no need for the veil after the crucifixion of Jesus. Acts 17 tells us that God no longer lives in temples made by hands, but dwells in those that are His. Jesus showed me that when the presence of God left the Tabernacle, it went into the hearts of all those who are His and the Spirit of God dwells in me. The temple in me has been gilded by the Holy Spirit with gold, and now it is my responsibility to decorate it for the God of all creation. Much like Solomon used precious stones to decorate the Holy place, we are to beautify our temple with the fruit of the Spirit; as listed in Galatians 5:22(KJV) love, joy, peace, long-suffering, gentleness, goodness, faith, meekness, and temperance.

Just as the priests did at Solomon's Tabernacle, our praise and worship of God will usher in His presence. When others see you, do they see the presence of God in your life? Is any wood, hay, or stubble found in the construction of your temple? Get on your knees before the Father, praying in the Spirit, and allow Him to show you the condition of your temple and what He desires to do in your life. Allow His presence to shine in you for others to see.

We give Him all praise and all glory.

29

Time

Time - *Indefinite continued progress of existence and events in the past, present and future regarded as a whole.*

> Genesis 1:1-5(KJV) – In the beginning God created the heaven and the earth. And the earth was without form, and void; and darkness was upon the face of the deep. And the Spirit of God moved upon the face of the waters. And God said, Let there be light: and there was light. And God saw the light, that it was good: and God divided the light from the darkness. And God called the light Day, and the darkness He called Night. And the evening and the morning were the first day.

And God created time. Time is something that happens when the past, the present and the future are all rolled into one. This body of Christ has been told before not to despise small beginnings. God's plan for us will develop in His time. But it is going to take time. We are young in Jesus for a season – that is the past. We don't see the end from the beginning; we don't see the past and we don't see the future – we are in the right now. King Solomon wrote in Ecclesiastes about the past and the future.

> Ecclesiastes 2:4-6(KJV) – I made me great works; I builded me houses; I planted me vineyards: I made me gardens and orchards, and I planted trees in them of all kind of fruits: I made me pools of water, to water therewith the wood that bringeth forth trees:

All of these Solomon did of his own will – not the will of the Father. He goes on to write about all the things he gathered, from servants, silver, gold, special treasures of kings, and great possessions. He says that he was great and had excelled more than all that went before him in Jerusalem. Whatsoever his eyes desired, he got it. I Kings 10 tells us that King Solomon received a tribute each year of 25 tons of gold, which in today's market is worth more than $1.3 billion dollars, which works out to about $3.5 million dollars a day. I suppose with all of that money at his disposal, he could buy whatever his eyes desired. After all was done, Solomon looked back over all he had accomplished with his work.

> Ecclesiastes 2:11(KJV) – Then I looked on all the works that my hands had wrought, and on the labour that I had laboured to do: and, behold, all was vanity and vexation of spirit, and there was no profit under the sun.

After all his labor had been accomplished, he looked back on it with all the hard work it took and found it fleeting, so useless and a chasing of the wind. Solomon had spent his days chasing after things of the world. Isn't that what we spend our days doing, chasing after the all-mighty dollar, working hard just to get ahead? All the things we gather in this world are fleeting. Then in chapter 3, it is revealed to Solomon there is a specific timing for every purpose under heaven.

> Ecclesiastes 3:11(KJV) – He hath made everything beautiful in His time: also He hath set the world in their heart, so that no man can find out the work that God maketh from the beginning to the end.

It is winter in north Texas right now and all the flowers have died back and the trees have lost their leaves. But we have the promise from God that spring will come, but we can't see it yet. We have the assurance that when it comes, it will bring colorful flowers on the plants and green leaves on the trees. But it will only be in God's timing; He has made everything beautiful in His time. We work in the present; you can't see what you will become and only from your memory can you remember the past. This is the day that the Lord has made, rejoice and be glad in it; don't wish you were in tomorrow or that you were back in the good old times. We don't know what is ahead for us.

> Isaiah 64:4(KJV) – For since the beginning of the world men have not heard, nor perceived by the ear, neither hath the eye seen, O God, beside thee, what He hath prepared for him that waiteth for Him.

God has plans for each of us that have yet come forth; plans from the beginning of creation. But notice the last four words of the scripture – that wait for Him; which is something we don't like to do. We are like King Solomon. Look what I did with my own hands; instead of waiting to see what God will do.

When I was young, I wanted to grow up to be a teacher. I have two younger sisters and we would play school every chance we got. Of course, I was always the teacher, as I was the oldest. After high school, I studied to get a degree in elementary education. But about halfway through college, Jesus directed my path another way. Even though I didn't become a teacher as a career, I found that in each of my jobs, I was using my teaching skills. Whether it be in training warehouse employees to ship merchandise, bookkeepers to use accounting programs, or the receptionist to answer the phone, my teaching talent was always being used. Even though society wouldn't label me as a teacher without the degree, I could still use my talent in the workforce. Then, about twelve years ago, Jesus opened the door for me to be a teacher of His Word. A very perceptive pastor could see the teaching gift in my life, what God destined for me from the beginning of time. He urged me – a little here and a little there to begin to walk in God's plans for my life. It took almost sixty years for that gift to develop and for Him to bring me forth and that long for me to grow into what Jesus has for me, to mature in my walk with Him. The last twelve years have been used to increase that talent for the Master's use. It is the timing of the Lord for my life. If I had tried to teach when I was 20 or 30, my teaching talent wouldn't have been complete. I had to sit back, wait on the Lord, and allow the Holy Spirit to speak into my life the Word of God.

> I Peter 5:6(KJV) – Humble yourselves therefore under the mighty hand of God, that He may exalt you in due time;

We cannot fulfill His calling with our own works, as King Solomon tried to do. He will bring His plan into its fullness in His way and at His time. The witness you will have will be so much greater in His appointed time. Just as Mordecai told Queen Esther in the book of Esther – who knows whether you are come to the kingdom for such a time as this?

We give Him all praise and all glory.

30

***

Obedience

Obedience – the act or practice of obeying; dutiful or submissive compliance. The trait of being willing to obey.

What is the last word of direction for your life that Jesus spoke? Were you faithful in following His instruction, no matter what it cost you? Did He require that you give up something that is very dear to you, something you loved with all your heart? The Bible is full of accounts of people who God instructed for their life and the consequences.

> Genesis 22:1-2(KJV) – And it came to pass after these things, that God did tempt Abraham, and said unto him, Abraham: and he said, Behold, here I am. And He said, Take now thy son, thine only son Isaac, whom thou lovest, and get thee into the land of Moriah; and offer him there for a burnt offering upon one of the mountains which I will tell thee of.

Isaac was the promised seed that God had foretold to Abraham and Sarah, the seed that would be as many as the stars. The son that Abraham and Sarah had prayed and believed in God for many years. And now God was telling Abraham to take his son, his only son, up the mountain and offer him there for a sacrificial offering. After receiving this word, I am sure that Abraham spent all night praying to make sure he heard God correctly, and then to bring his heart into submission to what God was directing. He had to believe in his heart that God's will would be done and that He would provide what is needful for His will. Abraham rose early and gathered all the items needed for the offering, including Isaac. After traveling for three days, they arrived at the place.

> Genesis 22:7-8(KJV) – And Isaac spake unto Abraham his father, and said, My father: and he said, Here am I, my son. And he said, Behold the fire and the wood: but where is the lamb for a burnt offering? And Abraham said, My son, God will provide Himself a lamb for a burnt offering: so they went both of them together.

I am sure all of Isaac's life, he had seen his father make burnt offerings unto the Lord and knew what it took in supplies. He saw the wood, the fire, and the knife, but nothing to sacrifice. As a result of Abraham spending time on his knees, he was assured in his heart that God knew how tough this command was for Abraham to fulfill and He would make provision. Now the time was getting critical, still, Abraham proceeded to build the altar, lay the wood in order, bind his son, and lay him on the altar upon the wood. Abraham took the last step and was ready with the knife to offer his son as a sacrifice. At this time, the angel of the Lord speaks from heaven.

> Genesis 22:12(KJV) – And he said, Lay not thine hand upon the lad, neither do thou any thing unto him: for now I know that thou fearest God, seeing thou hast not withheld thy son, thine only son from me.

Abraham looks up and sees a ram caught in a thicket by his horns. He took the ram and offered it as a burnt offering instead of his son. He obeyed unquestioningly the authority and knowledge of God. Abraham walked in the fulfilled promises for his life that God had made. He had a son, something he and Sarah had tried for years to conceive, with no results. But God promised, and the son was manifested. But this time, the temptation was a little more difficult to follow through, requiring more faith on Abraham's part.

Jesus speaks direction into each of our lives, allowing us the option to obey or to go our own way. Every time we don't do what Jesus tells us to do, we think we know better for our lives and are in disobedience. The prophet Samuel gave directions from the Lord to King Saul to destroy the Amalekites. God's instructions were for Saul's army to utterly destroy all that the Amalekites had, including all their animals, and spare them not. But Saul modified those orders a little. He decided to spare the king of the Amalekites and the best of their sheep, oxen, and lambs. When Samuel approached Saul regarding this action, Saul explained that the people had brought back the animals to offer as sacrifices to God.

> I Samuel 15:22-23(KJV) – And Samuel said, Hath the LORD as great delight in burnt offerings and sacrifices, as in obeying the voice of the LORD? Behold, to obey is better than sacrifice, and to hearken than the fat of rams. For rebellion is as the sin of witchcraft, and stubbornness is as iniquity and idolatry. Because thou hast rejected the word of the LORD, he hath also rejected thee from being king.

This wasn't the first time Saul had relied on his own council instead of obeying God. Saul usurped his authority, took on the priest's role as his own, and performed a ritual sacrifice. He had been given explicit directions from Samuel to wait seven days for him to arrive, and then the priests would perform the sacrifice. These seven days would have taught Saul patience and dependency upon God. Saul decided to take things into his own hands. Again, Saul blamed the people for his actions and felt like he couldn't wait. He will never know what God would have done for him had he waited. But Flesh wants what flesh wants. Why should he listen to God? After all, he was king over Israel? He was the top dog. Why did he have to obey what the prophet relayed from God? There are always consequences for disobeying, even for kings. God had David waiting in the wings, being prepared to take over Saul's place.

Not only are there consequences for not obeying God, there are blessings for being obedient. We have a bible full of instructions for our life that if we would just obey, the blessings would overtake us.

> Luke 6:38(KJV) – Give, and it shall be given unto you; good measure, pressed down, and shaken together, and running over, shall men give into your bosom. For with the same measure that ye mete withal it shall be measured to you again.

This is not a commandment that must be adhered to so that you can get more. This is about an attitude of the heart; allowing you to be a vessel God can use to bless others. If you freely, without thought of the return to you, give to others; in some form, it will come back to you. I Samuel tells us our disobedience to obey the voice of Jesus in our life is rebellion and stubbornness. There will be a battle between flesh and the Spirit of God within you when it comes to obedience. If you rely on flesh, it will be contrary to the moving of the Spirit.

Learning to obey the voice of God in your life is a step-by-step process. You will stumble and fall, but He is faithful and just to forgive us. Allow Abraham to be your example of how to walk in obedience and find the blessing of God in it, causing your faith to grow.

We give Him all praise and all glory.

31

Conviction

Conviction - *a formal declaration that someone is guilty of a sin, generally with a suggestion of shame of the person convicted.*

John wrote an account of Jesus going to the temple when the scribes and Pharisees brought before Him a woman caught in the act of adultery. They wanted to tempt Jesus by asking Him; since the Mosaic law says to stone her, what do You say? Jesus didn't answer them, He just stooped down and with His finger wrote on the ground. But this didn't seem to deter the scribes and the Pharisees, because they continued asking Him the same question. Jesus stood and said, Men in this group, if you are sinless, you may throw a stone at her. He then crouched down and continued writing on the ground.

John 8:9-11(KJV) – And they which heard it, being convicted by their own conscience, went out one by one, beginning at the eldest, even unto the last; and Jesus was left alone, and the woman standing in the midst. When Jesus had lifted up Himself, and saw none but the woman, He said unto her, Woman, where are those thine accusers? Hath no man condemned thee? She said, No man, Lord. And Jesus said unto her, Neither do I condemn thee: go, and sin no more.

John doesn't tell us what Jesus wrote on the ground, but whatever it was convicted the hearts of the men, probably bringing to memory all the sins that they had in their lives. The eldest leaving first, as I am sure his sins, those times he wandered from the path of uprightness and honor, were many. Jesus didn't yell at them, telling them they were sinners, condemning them for their actions. He didn't point out all the Mosaic laws they had broken, and no one had stoned them. He just reminded them that not one of them was without sin.

> Romans 3:23(KJV) – For all have sinned, and come short of the glory of God.

There is not one of us who can say we haven't sinned. But Jesus died for the remission of our sins. We are blessed to be able to ask for His forgiveness and we receive it. It is the Holy Spirit that convicts us when we stray from the path of uprightness and honor. The world will condemn you, but the Holy Spirit that dwells within you will convict you.

> Romans 8:1(KJV) – There is therefore now no condemnation to them which are in Christ Jesus, who walk not after the flesh, but after the Spirit.

So, if you are walking after the Spirit and not after the flesh, you don't have to accept condemnation for your life. The enemy delights in whispering condemning words in your ear, but you don't have to agree or believe it.

If you look at the life of Job in the Old Testament, you will see that he was a righteous man before God. He had a wife, many sons and daughters, servants, and large herds of sheep, camels, and oxen. He had been blessed of God because of his righteousness and faithfulness.

God allowed Satan to test Job, to prove that a righteous man would still be faithful no matter what the circumstances. Job loses his children and his possessions; becoming very ill with boils and sores. His three friends come to visit him in his saddened state and for seven days sit in mourning with Job. Then at the end of the seven days, each friend begins to speak why he felt that God had caused this to happen in Job's life. Each claiming that surely there was sin in Job's life and God was punishing him for the unrighteous act that had clearly been done. They were saying God was condemning Job. But Job knew in his heart he was a blameless man; what his friends were accusing him of was just not true. Just as the scribes and Pharisees in the scripture from John, Job's friends didn't have all the facts to be condemning him. They didn't know the will of God for Job's life, just as we don't know the will of God for anyone's life but our own.

Condemnation doesn't mean we are sentencing someone to death by stoning them. It means the expression of very strong disapproval toward someone; which we are all guilty of doing. It is easy to look at someone else and speak words of judgment about them, putting them on trial and condemning them for their actions. I live in a small rural town and I use the Postal service to bring a lot of my packages to me. Over the last few years, I have become acquainted with one particular postal delivery man. He is very personable and always delivers with a smile in a timely manner. This week we had a different Postal delivery person. I was expecting a couple of packages to be delivered and I had three packages to be picked up so I was keenly aware when she came by much later than normal. When she finally showed up, she only delivered one of my packages. She then returned thirty minutes later with my additional package and a letter, apologizing for being so late. After she left, I guess you could say I voiced my strong disapproval of having a new postal person because she just seemed so inept and I wanted our previous one back. Later it was brought to my attention that she left her route and drove over to the Post Office to drop off the packages that were being sent out so they would be post marked that day. She went above and beyond what was asked of her. Conviction from the Holy Spirit hit my heart, and I repented for my attitude. Jesus saved me from opening my mouth and voicing my disapproval to the tardy postal person, but the attitude was in my heart.

Matthew 7:1(KJV) – Judge not, that ye be not judged.

In all three examples covered here, someone took it upon themselves to be the judge for another's life. That word 'judge' in this scripture is translated condemn. If you are judging someone, you have the same heart as the scribes and Pharisees that approached Jesus. Condemnation is of the world. Conviction is of God. We must be sensitive to the Holy Spirit when it speaks conviction into our heart and not listen to the condemnation from the world.

We give Him all praise and all glory.

32

Prayer

Prayer – a solemn request for help or expression of thanks addressed to God.

Prayer is a very integral part of our walk with God. It is the direct line of communication we have with Him and, as with all relationships, continuous contact is very important. Even though Matthew 6:8(KJV) says Your Father knoweth what ye have need of, before ye ask Him; Philippians 4:6(KJV) says – Be careful for nothing; but in every thing by prayer and supplication with thanksgiving let your requests be made known unto God. So, if He knows what we need, why should we have to pray about everything? Why couldn't He just give us what is lacking in our lives? God didn't create robots. He created man in His own image; to be more like Him than anything else in all that He created. And He gave man a living soul; capable of reasoning and making decisions in his own mind, knowing that His creation wouldn't always choose the correct path. But He also gave us a way to talk to Him, to voice our feelings, hurts, wants, needs, joys, thanksgivings, and all the other emotions we have. I hear you saying – I have tried praying, but He didn't answer. I didn't hear Him say anything to me. God has a divine plan for each of us, but He won't force it on us. It is our assignment to seek Him and allow Him to work it out in our lives. So, we must pray.

> James 5:16(KJV) – Confess your faults one to another and pray one for another, that ye may be healed. The effectual fervent prayer of a righteous man availeth much.

Many times, when we read this scripture, we focus on the words effectual and fervent. The word to look at is righteous; what is your standing with God? When we go to God in prayer in the name of Jesus, we should first be going with a repentant heart, confessing any transgressions that would keep us out of His presence. James wrote in this scripture to the body of Christ, to own up to their mistakes and faults. I John 1:9(KJV) tells us – if we confess our sins, He is faithful and just to forgive us our sins, and to cleanse us from all unrighteousness. Realizing the many times we didn't follow God's direction; or didn't grasp His will for our lives, will be a preparation to obey the next time. If we want our prayers to be effectual and fervent, we must cleanse our hearts of all unrighteousness. This will allow us to approach the throne of God with a repentant heart, to open the flow between you and Him.

> James 4:2-3(KJV) – Ye lust, and have not: ye kill, and desire to have, and cannot obtain: ye fight and war, yet ye have not, because ye ask not. Ye ask, and receive not, because ye ask amiss, that ye may consume it upon your lusts.

James is telling us that when we are envious of what others have, we think vicious thoughts against them. We want something we can't have, covet something that belongs to someone else, and we plot on how we will get it. We are in this predicament because we didn't ask God. And then when we do ask; we still don't get it, because of the attitude of our heart. We live in a time of self-indulgence; where everything is all about me. But Jesus is looking for those with a heart toward all people. As we read in James 5, we are to pray for one another. Jesus also taught that we are to pray for our enemies.

> Matthew 5:43-44(KJV) – Ye have heard that it hath been said, Thou shalt love thy neighbour, and hate thine enemy. But I say unto you, Love your enemies, bless them that curse you, do good to them that hate you, and pray for them which despitefully use you, and persecute you;

Jesus was telling them it was easy to pray for someone who was a Jew, but could you pray for the Gentiles or Samaritans? Could you pray for someone of another denomination or even someone who didn't believe in Jesus? I find it is easy to pray for my neighbor, my friends, and family when the opportunity arises; but it takes an attitude adjustment of my carnal self to pray for my enemies. In surrendering to the move of the Holy Ghost in my life and taking on a Christ-like attitude by praying for my enemies, I will be acting as a true son of my Father. He is good to the evil and the upright, the just and the unjust. There are so many people lost in this battle of good and evil that the only hope they have is our praying against the wiles of the enemy for their lives. Romans 8:26(KJV) tells us that we know not what we should pray for as we ought; but the Spirit itself makes intercession for us with groanings which cannot be uttered. I allow the Holy Spirit to intercede for them by praying in tongues as the Spirit of God gives utterance; that way I know I am praying the will of God for their lives.

After your heart is in the proper attitude with God and you have prayed for all that, He has placed on your heart, you are now in a position to pray for yourself; not praying for wants or even needs, but praying for the perfect will of God to be done in your life. No one knows the will of God for you, but the Father. Jesus gave His disciples a simple prayer.

Matthew 9:10(KJV) – Thy kingdom come. Thy will be done in earth, as it is in heaven.

God's will for each of us has already been established in heaven; so, our prayer should be that His will would be manifested in earth; not the green ball we live on, but in His temple that resides in each of us. If we allow His will to become our own will; that we align up to what He has for our lives, our walk is so much easier. I have found for my life that God takes care of all my needs if I pray that His will be done in my life and surrender to Him. I can then witness the goodness of God for my life because He provides everything I need. Prayer helps you grow in faith and walk in wisdom. We can't live by what we see; but by the moving of the Spirit in our lives. Allow the Holy Spirit to lead you in your prayer life; that the effectual fervent prayers of a righteous man will avail much.

We give Him all praise and all glory.

33

Ear

Ear – an ability to recognize sounds, especially language.

What has Jesus spoken into your life recently? Have you been able to recognize His voice; did you take time to let Him speak? Jesus used the phrase "he that hath ears to hear, let him hear" many times in teaching His parables to the crowds. In Mark, He began teaching by the seaside, and a great multitude gathered around. He taught the parable of the sowing of the seed. The sower sowed the seed with one of them falling on hard soil and a bird came down and snapped it up. Another seed fell on rocky ground where the soil was thin, so it sprang up quickly. Then the hot sun came out; causing the small plant to wither and die. One seed fell among the weeds, that grew tall and choked the seedling to yield no fruit. The final seed fell on good ground; it grew tall and produced fruit, some thirty, and some sixty, and some a hundredfold. He ended His teaching with Mark 4:9(KJV) He that hath ears to hear, let him hear. After Jesus finished, the crowds dispersed and He was left alone with the disciples and a few others; they asked Him why He taught in parables instead of explaining what He said more clearly.

Mark 4:11-12(KJV) – And He said unto them, Unto you it is given to know the mystery of the kingdom of God: but unto them that are without, all these things are done in parables: That seeing they may see, and not perceive; and hearing they may hear, and not understand; lest at any time they should be converted, and their sins should be forgiven them.

Jesus was not saying that they couldn't hear the audible words spoken, but that they didn't have the teachable heart to receive the principles of His parables. He goes on to explain the meaning of the parable to those who are with Him.

Mark 4:13-14(KJV) – And He said unto them, Know ye not this parable? And how then will ye know all parables? The sower soweth the word.

Jesus knew that the explanation of identifying the sower sowing the word cleared up the understanding of the parable. The crowd who Jesus was teaching were mostly farmers and understood all about seeds and sowing. It is the word of God that is being sewn into the hearts of men. If the word was received in the heart, that was the fertile ground where the seed could be watered and nourished to bring forth some thirty, some sixty, and some a hundredfold. The word could fall on a hard heart and the enemy will come and snatch it up. It could fall on a heart that is filled with the cares of the world, not allowing the word to grow but to cutting off fruit. Have you ever read scriptures in the Bible that didn't make sense at the time? Then at the appointed time of the Father, the Holy Spirit gives you the understanding? Those scriptures are the seed being planted in your heart and at the perfect timing of the Father it will be revealed to you what was truly meant by the scriptures. Jesus doesn't expect us to understand everything in the

Bible at once, He gives it to us line upon line, here a little and there a little.

Have you ever been in a conversation with someone, listening to the words coming from their mouths but not really hearing them, too busy thinking of something else to hear what they say? Then suddenly, you hear your name because they are trying to get your attention. It is like all the words just flew over your head and didn't sink in. Many times that is how we are with our Father. We sit in the pew at church, listening to the pastor or the teacher, but not hearing a word they say; when we should be taking notes, concentrating on the words that are being spoken, allowing the Holy Spirit to plant the seeds of the word in our hearts. It isn't until God calls our name that we stop to hear what He has to say. Listening is hearing all the noises going on around you, while hearing is the ability to grasp the words that are being spoken. We must develop our ability to hear the voice of God instead of listening to all the surrounding sounds. Jesus will speak to us in a language we can understand; when He called Simon Peter, He told him he would be a fisher of men. Peter understood because his trade was sea fishing.

Our prayers should continually be: Father, open my ears to hear and my heart to receive. God gave instructions to Ezekiel in Ezekiel 3:10(KJV) - all My words that I shall speak unto thee receive in thine heart and hear with thine ears. The word 'hear' is translated in the Hebrew, meaning to hear intelligently with the intention of obedience. It was important that Ezekiel hear the words of God spoken concerning the children of Israel in order to prophesy to them. The Israelites could not hear the word of God for themselves, so Ezekiel needed to be obedient to what he heard and relay it to the people. But we have the ability to hear the voice of God and we have the written word of God for instruction in our lives.

We must allow God to speak into our lives to grow in Him. In my studies of the word of God, each week the 'word' for that week comes as a still small voice from Him. The seed of the word is planted in my heart, to be watered, nurtured, and protected for it to produce to its potential. But it takes me hearing the word spoken and not just listening to all the sounds going on around me; trying to decipher on my own which word came from God. At the beginning of the week, the word starts out small, with just a few leaves coming from the sprout. Then, as I keep my ears open and my heart ready to receive, I receive confirmations of the word in different ways. The more I allow the Holy Spirit to guide me in writing the word by following the direction He purposes the more I hear what is desired to be written. When Jesus said in Mark 4:9(KJV) - He that hath ears to hear, let him hear, He didn't say that only a few chosen ones could hear. He said that all could hear, if they had ears to hear. Meaning, if you have a heart that is willing and ready to receive, you will hear His voice speaking into your life. We don't want to be in a position where we hear and don't understand what He is saying. Not only is it important that we know the sound of His voice when He speaks to us, but we must also have our heart in a receptive attitude to receive the word and the obedience to do as He tells us.

We give Him all praise and all glory.

34

Balance

Balance – *an even distribution of weight enabling someone or something to remain upright and steady.*

In biblical times, scales and balances were used as a method of measuring bulk items; making it the way people bought and sold. The cunning merchants had figured out how to cheat in their trading by using false weights in their scales. Thus, swindling the people out of their just payment. In Leviticus, God tells the children of Israel His opinion of these false representations.

> Leviticus 19:35-36(KJV) - Ye shall do no unrighteousness in judgment, in meteyard, in weight, or in measure. Just balances, just weights, a just ephah, and a just hin, shall ye have: I am the Lord your God, which brought you out of the land of Egypt.

The trade merchants used a scale to measure the dry and liquid goods with weights to determine quantity and value. As there was no standardized weighing system, each merchant could falsify his measuring tools as he wanted. God is telling them that they are to not only be just in the weights and measures of items, but in the judgment of others. He described each of these measures as just; meaning that it is altogether right in both the moral and legal setting. This is a type and shadow of the principle in the New Testament Jesus taught.

> Matthew 7:2(KJV) - For with what judgment ye judge, ye shall be judged: and with what measure ye mete, it shall be measured to you again.

In the Old Testament, Daniel wrote of the dream he interpreted for King Belshazzar. It all started when the king had a great feast; inviting his princes, his wives, and his concubines. They used the gold and silver vessels Nebuchadnezzar had taken from the temple in Jerusalem to make a royal toast. They drank wine; and praised the idol gods of gold, and of silver, of brass, of iron, of wood, and of stone. During their revelry, fingers of a man's hand came forth, and wrote on the king's palace wall. The king saw what the hand wrote and his countenance changed, so much so that his knees started knocking. He called for all his astrologers, all the wise men in the kingdom; promising them whoever reads the writing on the wall with interpretation will receive a purple robe of royal honor, a gold chain around his neck, and shall be the third ruler in the kingdom. (Belshazzar's father was the first ruler and Belshazzar was the second ruler.). But the king's wise men could not only interpret the meaning of what was written, they couldn't even read it. That revelation made the king even more troubled. The queen, seeing that the king's countenance had changed, reminded him of the man in the kingdom who had the spirit of the Holy Gods. This man had the understanding and wisdom of the gods. She reminded Belshazzar that this wise man had interpreted a dream for Nebuchadnezzar, the king's forefather, and was rewarded the position of the chief of the magicians, astrologers, and soothsayers. The man referenced was Daniel. He was called to come before the king, who explained the situation that no one could interpret the words written on the wall. The king offered him the same gifts that he offered the others, but Daniel said no thank you, but I will read the writing and tell you what it means. Daniel told the king he had not humbled his heart, but had lifted up himself against the Lord of heaven. Also, he brought the vessels of God's house in and used them to drink wine while praising the idol gods of silver, gold, brass, iron, wood, and stone. He didn't glorify God in whose hand his breath is. Then Daniel read what was written and gave the interpretation.

> Daniel 5:25-28(KJV) - And this is the writing that was written, MENE, MENE, TEKEL, UPHARSIN. This is the interpretation of the thing: MENE; God hath numbered thy kingdom, and finished it. TEKEL; Thou art weighed in the balances, and art found wanting. PERES; Thy kingdom is divided, and given to the Medes and Persians.

God is telling Belshazzar that he has been weighed on the scales of righteousness and come up lacking. He was also told that God numbered his kingdom, meaning that his days to rule Babylon were finite and were coming to an end; telling Belshazzar that he was not all he thought he was. He had allowed the things of the world to pull him off balance in God's scale and become deficient. On that night, Belshazzar the king was slain and the Medes took over the kingdom. The hand of God was taken off his life.

In the natural, we try to live a balanced life of our own making. We propose to eat a balanced diet to keep our body functioning at its fullest capacity. We monitor our financial accounts to make sure they balance with the banks and lending institutions. Seeking a balance of our time between work and leisure is important. It is difficult to keep all of these balancing activities in place without the indwelling of the Holy Ghost. Jesus tells us in Matthew that we have a choice of two paths that we can walk down, but we can only take one path.

> Matthew 7:13-14(KJV) – Enter ye in at the strait gate: for wide is the gate, and broad is the way, that leadeth to destruction, and many there be which go in thereat: Because strait is the gate, and narrow is the way, which leadeth unto life, and few there be that find it.

The wide path is easy and has many, many people on it; but it leads to death. You walk a narrow path when you follow Jesus, that leads to life. This road is hard to find and few discover it. Walking the narrow road with Jesus is much like walking a balance beam in gymnastics. There are deep perils on each side; if you fall off one way, you fall back into the sin of the world and if you fall off the other way, you fall into legalism. Are you going to be like Belshazzar; weighed off balance on God's scale and found lacking? It is only with the grace of God dwelling in each of us that we are able to maneuver and keep our balance on the path that He chose for us. Ask the Holy Spirit to reveal the edges of the path to you; so you can keep going the narrow way.

We give Him all praise and all glory.

36

Worship

Worship – the feeling or expression of reverence and adoration for God

John 4:23-24 – But the hour cometh, and now is, when the true worshippers shall worship the Father in spirit and in truth: for the Father seeketh such to worship Him. God is a Spirit: and they that worship Him must worship Him in spirit and in truth.

The word 'worship' in Greek comes from a word meaning to kiss like a dog licking his master's hand. The act of kissing one's hand has been around since about the 8th century. It is a sign of love, respect, and devotion to that person. Although we can't actually kiss God's hand, we can come to Him in an attitude of obedience, commitment, and reverence. Obedience, as if our head is bowed over His hand, showing Him the respect He is due. Commitment, in that we are dedicated to Him no matter the tests or trials that we go through. Reverence is our deep respect for Him, for who He is in our lives, and for what He has done for us. The scripture says – they that worship Him must worship Him in spirit and in truth. We are told we must worship God from our spirit, from our hearts, not our heads. Jesus told us in John 14:6(KJV) –

I am the way, the truth, and the life: no man cometh unto the Father, but by me.

In this scripture in John 14, Jesus has just ministered to the woman at the well. She told Him that she saw that He was a prophet because He knew personal things about her. She said, "Our fathers worshipped in this mountain and you, as a Jew, say that is not the place to worship and that we should worship in Jerusalem". Jesus goes on to tell her that it is not the place where she worships that is important, but how she worships; is her worship done in the Spirit and is it real? Our worship must be directed toward God and done by the indwelling of the Holy Spirit and the truth of God that has been revealed to us. God is looking for those who will worship Him in spirit and in truth.

In the II Chronicles, Hezekiah was made king of Israel and reigned in Jerusalem. His father, Ahaz, reigned before him and had trashed the temple of God. In the first year of Hezekiah's reign, he commissioned the temple to be cleaned out and restored to what it had been. He had the Levites purify and sanctify it. Their instructions were not to be negligent in their cleaning; for the Lord had chosen them to stand before Him, to serve Him, and that they should minister to God. So, the Levites went into the temple and cleaned out all the filth, the evidence of idols to other gods, and threw it away. When the temple was clean, they reported back to Hezekiah all that they had done. The Levites had even prepared the rams, lambs, and goats for the altar sacrifice. When the Levites began sacrificing the animals, making atonement for the sins of Israel, King Hezekiah called forth all of those with the instruments of David and the priests with the trumpets. These burnt offerings symbolized the total commitment and surrender to God for the people of Israel.

II Chronicles 29:27b-30(KJV) - And when the burnt offering began, the song of the Lord began also with the trumpets, and the instruments ordained by David king of Israel. And all the congregation worshipped, and the singers sang, and the trumpeters sounded: and all this continued until the burnt offering was finished. And when they had made an end of offering, the king and all that were present with him bowed themselves, and worshipped. Moreover, Hezekiah the king and the princes commanded the Levites to sing praise unto the Lord with the words of David, and of Asaph the seer. And they sang praises with gladness, and they bowed their heads and worshipped.

These scriptures show the children of Israel both praising and worshipping God. This is a type and shadow of what Jesus is doing in our hearts, to prepare us to worship God in spirit and in truth. He has come into our hearts to clean out all the idols that have been placed there by us. Then He made the ultimate sacrifice for our sins by dying on the cross. Now He has brought forth the instruments of praise to lead us into the worship of the only true God. Too many times, the words praise and worship are put together as the same act. But there is a difference between these two actions. Praise is thanking God for what He has done in your life; standing in awe that He has chosen you and is working through you to reach others. Praise prepares your heart for worship and ushers in the Holy Spirit to bring you into the presence of God. Worship comes from the indwelling of the Holy Spirit and is intimate between you and God.

Psalms 24:3-5(KJV) – Who shall ascend into the hill of the Lord? Or who shall stand in His holy place? He that hath clean hands, and a pure heart; who hath not lifted up his soul unto vanity, nor sworn deceitfully. He shall receive the blessing from the Lord, and righteousness from the God of his salvation.

Who is worthy of coming into the presence of God? Only those who do not rely on their works, but on their walk of faith, to obtain a meeting with God, to come into His presence. You can't just be a good man or a good woman, you must have a heart that has been purged from evil and pure before God. Do we worship Him with the help of the Holy Spirit? Praise is different than worship. We can't enter into worship except by the spirit of praise, because praise brings to memory all the wonderful things that God has done for each of us. John wrote in the book of Revelation what he saw in heaven of the worship that is ever going forth there.

> Revelation 4:8-11(KJV) – And the four beasts had each of them six wings about him; and they were full of eyes within: and they rest not day and night, saying, Holy, Holy, Holy, Lord God Almighty, which was, and is, and is to come. And when those beasts give glory and honour and thanks to Him that sat on the throne, who liveth for ever and ever, the four and twenty elders fall down before Him that sat on the throne, and worship Him that liveth for ever and ever, and cast their crowns before the throne saying, Thou art worthy, O Lord, to receive glory and honour and power: for Thou hast created all things, and for thy pleasure they are and were created.

Note that neither of these two worship songs contains the words I, me, or my. In my prayer life, I have found it helpful to get into the spirit of worship by quoting the songs that are being sung in heaven. This conditions my heart to come into the presence of God and minister to

Him. Add these to your daily prayers and see the Holy Spirit usher you into the presence of God.

We give Him all praise and all glory.

38

Praise

Praise – *to express warm approval or admiration of*

In studying the word praise for this week, I found in the book of Psalms, that the word praise in English was translated into at least five different Hebrew words. We are going to look at the word 'halal', which means to boast or to rave.

> Psalms 22:22(KJV) – I will declare Thy name unto my brethren: in the midst of the congregation will I praise Thee.

In this psalm of David, he is telling God that he would describe in detail God's reputation, God's fame, and God's glory to his brothers or those that were of a like mind. So, he was going to boast of the goodness of God. We all have friends who have something to boast about every time we see them. Their kids have just gotten an award for being the best at some sporting events. Their job just gave them a new promotion with a raise that is just AMAZING!! When was the last time you boasted about what Jesus was doing in your life? Have you raved about the goodness of the Lord to anyone lately? This word will be a little different this time. I am going to praise God for the things He is doing in and through my life. I am boasting about His goodness to me.

However, sometimes it is difficult to praise God where He has you. You don't feel comfortable and what He is asking of you doesn't come naturally. About thirty years ago, my husband and I were seeking God for the church He would plant us in. We were introduced to a prophet of God and his family. They were starting a new church and we felt led to attend. After a few years of sitting under the Word of God being taught, the prophet asked me to come up and give a word from Jesus, even if it was just one word. That was the beginning of a journey that led to the calling of God for my life as a teacher. But it was definitely a stretching for me. I am not much of a talker, much less stand up in front of people and speak. And in taking the baby steps at the beginning, I began to understand how Jesus would use me. He has to stretch each of us out of our comfort zone for us to come to the place where we can praise Him. In Isaiah, God is talking to the children of Israel concerning being stretched out in their comfort zone.

Isaiah 54:1-2(KJV) – Sing, O barren, thou that didst not bear; break forth into singing, and cry aloud, thou that didst not travail with child: for more the children of the desolate than the children of the married wife, saith the Lord. Enlarge the place of thy tent, and let them stretch forth the curtains of thine habitations: spare not, lengthen thy cords, and strengthen thy stakes;

Through Isaiah, the Lord is saying don't look at what you don't have in your life, because there is going to be an increase in you. Praise Him wherever He has you by allowing there to be more of Him and less of you. Just imagine what it would be like with Jesus using you on a much larger scale than you are walking in right now.

We must be sensitive to the Holy Spirit working in us, allowing Him to do His perfect will in us, praising Him along the way. If you don't want to enlarge your tent and allow God to use you in His plan, don't worry; God will find someone who is willing to take your place. In the book of Esther, that is what Mordecai had to remind Esther when she was reluctant to go to the king to plead for the safety of the Jewish people. Who knows whether you are coming to the kingdom for such a time as this? Being stretched allowed Esther's faith to undergo what lay ahead that she felt unprepared for.

I find this lesson to be timely for my life and what Jesus is doing in and through me. It would be really easy for me to sit in a pew and listen. Oh, I would pray and I would sing praises to Him, but don't make me get up in front of people and speak. But in Matthew 28 – Jesus tells us to Go and teach all nations. You don't have to go to Africa unless Jesus tells you, but your nation could be that lady next door or someone who works with you who needs a word from the Lord. A few years ago, I received a prophecy from Jesus for my life. He said – "Now is your greatest hour. I have a work for you. I say go." It has taken a few years to get everything in place for this prophecy to come forth; both in me and in others He is working in. But I can see His hand in my life and I am definitely having to enlarge my tent to make room for all He is doing. He wants us to take our witness out to others in the marketplace and how can you do that if you stay in your small little tent? Allow Jesus to show you how to enlarge your tent and stretch your cords, while continuing to praise Him. Maybe you will be the next leader of a nation or He will use you to lead a mighty move of God. We must be adaptable to stretch and move with what Jesus is doing in the days to come. Don't get comfortable in the place you are in. Things are not going to stay the same as we now know it. God is going to expand His presence on the earth thru the Holy Spirit and we must be ready to praise Him for whatever He has for us.

We give Him all praise and all glory.

39

First fruits

First fruits – *the first of any increase received, usually but not limited to financial gain, given to God as an offering.*

Do you ever come across a verse of scripture that you have never noticed before? You know you have read that chapter in the Bible, but you must have read right through this one. The verse for today was read by my pastor during a service recently and it tugged on my heart. It didn't jump off the page at me; however, it is a hidden truth that we need to study. So, we are going to take a close look at what is being said. In the New Testament book he wrote, James is writing to the twelve tribes of Israel which are the Christians spread among the Gentile countries. After Jesus was crucified, many of the disciples went up into what is now Turkey as missionaries. James is writing to those churches that have been planted by the disciples. The churches must have been going through tests and trials because of their faith, but James is reminding them that the trying of their faith produces patience.

James 1:17-18(KJV) – Every good gift and every perfect gift is from above, and comes down from the Father of lights, with whom is no variableness, neither shadow of turning. Of His own will begat He us with the word of truth, that we should be a kind of firstfuits of His creatures.

That the God we serve is steadfast and consistent; He doesn't change His mind and turn to go the other way. It was God's divine purpose, His own will, to create us. Genesis 2:7(KJV) says; And the LORD GOD formed man of the dust of the ground, and breathed into his nostrils the breath of life; and man became a living soul. In Genesis 1 everything God created was spoken into existence by the words of His mouth, but Chapter 2 tells us He molded us, He squeezed us into shape much as a potter molds his clay. He knelt down in the dirt and formed each of us with His hands. So, you can see that He created us differently from any other thing that He spoke into existence and we are precious to Him. He then gave this treasured form He molded CPR and breathed the breath of life into his nostrils, awakening his soul. All animals have the breath of life in them, but we are the only creation that God went a step further and gave us a spirit. When we receive the Holy Spirit with evidence of speaking in tongues, God breathes the word of truth into our spirit, revealing the mysteries of the scriptures to us. So, in the first part of the scripture James is telling the churches, it was God's divine purpose to create man, not only breathing into his nostrils the breath of life; but also to make available the interpretation of the word of truth, His written Word, through the indwelling of the Holy Spirit. I think the enemy beats us down sometimes and we fail to remember how precious we are to our Heavenly Father, and how much He loves each of us. Think about the things in this world that are precious to you; your children, relationships, and mementos of those who are no longer with you. What would you be willing to give up for another person? John 3:16(KJV) says; For God so loved the world, that He gave His only begotten Son. God loves all those He begat, all those He molded from clay and breathed life into; so much so He was willing to sacrifice His only Son on the cross for their sins.

There is a purpose for God's will in each of our lives. We are called to be His first fruits. The Gentile churches could relate to what James was writing to them concerning first fruits, as they were an agricultural community. Even though they were Gentiles and not Jews, they understood the meaning of first fruits. The second half of the scripture says that we should be a kind of first fruits of His creatures. Old Testament Jews were taught to give first fruits each season for a sacrifice. When Moses came down the mountain after getting the Ten Commandments, God also gave Moses laws for the children of Israel. These included laws concerning acts of violence, the responsibility of owners, restitution, and human relations. Then He told Moses to set up three appointed feasts and what offerings were to be brought for the feasts.

> Exodus 23:19(KJV) – The first of the first fruits of thy land thou shalt bring into the house of the LORD thy GOD.

Moses had just led the children of Israel out of Egyptian captivity. They had been accustomed to living on just what they had. But now they weren't slaves any longer and would be living off the land, having crops and herds. They were instructed to bring in the very first fruits from their harvest to God as an offering. This was a form of worship to God, displaying to Him that the Israelites trusted His provision from the remainder of the crops. Being obedient to the instructions of God, in Exodus 23:25(KJV) He promises, And ye shall serve the Lord your God, and He shall bless thy bread, and thy water. With this promise, He would make provision for them in their submission to Him. First fruits are not just an Old Testament tenet. Jesus is a type and shadow of the first fruits of God.

I Corinthians 15:20(KJV) – But now is Christ risen from the dead, and become the first fruits of them that slept.

Jesus gave us a pattern for our lives. Have you ever wondered why you are here? Why were you born at this time, and in this place? Could it be that in God's will, now is the time and place for you to be and He has a divine plan for your life to bring you to the best you can be? That you would be able to give a testimony of the goodness of God to those who are not filled with His word of truth. The Israelites gave the first of their crops, their herds, and anything else they produced to be sacrificed to God. God created us as His first fruit. We are the best thing He created and He offered it up. We should follow this action and do the same. We are blessed with a new 24 hours each day. We should give first fruits of our time. Don't put off reading your bible and praying until you have completed everything else in your day. Make the time spent with God top on your schedule. Don't put the talents He has placed in you at the bottom of your list to use for His ministry. Don't let your job, your friends, all the chores you have to do at home or anything else get ahead of what you should be doing for God. He has placed that talent in you for a purpose and that is to be a first fruit sacrifice unto Him. We should be developing these talents faithfully so that when the appointed time comes, He can use us. If you receive some unexpected money, you should give of that increase, not as a tithe but as a sacrifice unto God. Any increase in your life is an area to bring first fruits into the kingdom. Put first things first in your life.

Proverbs 3:9(KJV) – Honor the Lord with thy substance, and with the first fruits of all thine increase.

We give Him all praise and all glory.

40

Persistent

Persistent – to continue firmly in a course of action in spite of difficulty or opposition

Is there anything in your life that you are persistent about? Maybe you are anticipating a promotion in your job that you are not quite qualified to take. You have worked hard and been diligent with everything you have been given at work; hoping your actions will bring forth the fruit of an advancement. You expect that your attentive and relentless efforts to work through all the difficulties and oppositions thrown your way will pay off and your goal will be accomplished. Even though there are probably others being considered for the position who are more qualified, you hope your persistence will be rewarded. Or maybe you are trying to lose those last few pounds that just seem to hang on. You have faithfully watched what you eat, not necessarily counting calories, but changing your eating habits for a healthier lifestyle transformation. You have added daily exercise to your routine and all these changes seem to be in vain. But you are persistent about staying on course; resisting all the sugary temptations that come in front of you, knowing that results don't happen overnight. Why is it that no matter the objective you are pursuing in your natural life, you don't apply the same persistence to your relationship with God? You have prayed and prayed about a situation and nothing happened like you thought it would. Do you just give up? How determined are you to understand the will of God for your life? We should be as tenacious in this pursuit as we are in everything in our natural life that we are chasing. Paul wrote to the church at Thessalonica instructions for their walk in God.

> I Thessalonians 5:17-18(KJV) – Pray without ceasing. In every thing give thanks: for this is the will of God in Christ Jesus concerning you.

The word 'ceasing' in Greek means without intermission or a break. I know, you are saying how can I pray without ceasing if I have to work, take care of a family, and do everything that needs to be done in my life. You must realize that the word 'pray' doesn't mean you have to bow your head and say the Lord's prayer continually. Pray, in this instance, means to worship God in everything; giving Him praise persistently as you walk about your day; which includes all the good times and the bad times. With the same determination that you used to change your eating habits, you should also apply to your attitude of praise toward the Father for all things, as this is His will for your life. So, as you walk through the tests, trials, and triumphs that occur in what you do, your attitude should be "Thank you, Jesus." No matter what the conditions are. Just as persistence in your eating habit change will bring forth a healthier body, the same persistence applied to your walk with Jesus will result in a healthier relationship with God.

It is a hot summer in North Texas and the flower beds in front of my house are full of shrubs and plants that need water. So, every day I turn on the watering system to give them a drink. But not only do they get a drink, but all the weeds that have decided to take root come forth as well. No matter how many of these pesky weeds I pull, more seem to keep coming and try to choke out the life of the plants. Who knew weeds could be so persistent? The same goes for the weeds that the enemy plants in our spirit. Maybe yours is the same as mine right now, saying that I will never accomplish the plans God has for my life; attacking my confidence that He will do what He promised. I just speak the Word into my life – I John. 5:14(KJV) – And this is the confidence that we have in Him, that, if we ask any thing according to His will, He heareth us. Those words feed my spirit while pulling out the weed, but I realize that some of the roots may still be there. Every time that thought comes; I speak the Word of God into it with determination. By doing so, my faith that God will perform His word in my life and eventually the Word will kill the spirit of doubt that would like to take over. But don't get excited; thinking that all the weeds are out of your spirit. You just pulled one weed and, like in my natural flowerbed, there are a multitude of bothersome weeds trying to take over. Don't get discouraged and don't look at the circumstances. We need to take each weed to God as they come up, realizing just like in the natural, there will always be weeds. There are some buried so deep that it takes the Light of the Countenance of God to reveal them.

Psalm 90:8(KJV) – Thou hast set our iniquities before Thee, our secret sins in the light of Thy countenance.

Our iniquities, our secret heart and its sins which we would so like to conceal even from ourselves; He has set them in the revealing light of His countenance. We all have thoughts and attitudes that don't line up with the word of God, things we won't even admit to ourselves. At the appointed time of the Father, He will bring them to our attention, shining the light of His countenance on them. God will deal with those weeds in His time. We just need to be persistent in allowing Him to make our heart pure.

There are times when it is not convenient to be tenacious with what God is doing in your life. In the book of Daniel, we are told how he was captured by the Babylonian king when he was a young man. He and three of his Jewish friends lived their exiled lives in the court of the king. Over the years, Daniel had several encounters with King Nebuchadnezzar, which included interpreting dreams and visions plus walking through the fiery furnace. Daniel was shown to be wiser than all the astrologers, soothsayers, and the Chaldeans through his God-given wisdom. He was rewarded by being made the first president over all the rulers of the kingdom. All the Babylonian presidents, princes, governors, and captains had to report and give account to a Jewish man. They didn't like the situation and plotted to kill him; by convincing the king to make a new royal statute. This new law stated that anyone who requests a petition of any God or man for a period of thirty days, except the king, shall be cast in the den of lions. The king signed the writing and the decree. Daniel's enemies knew they could catch him disobeying this law. However, Daniel had not been known to follow man; but to listen to the leading of his God.

> Daniel 6:10(KJV) – Now when Daniel knew that the writing was signed, he went into his house; and his windows being open in his chamber toward Jerusalem, he kneeled upon his knees three times a day, and prayed, and gave thanks before his God, as he did aforetime.

Daniel didn't go in front of the king and complain about the new law. He didn't remind the king of all the signs and wonders that Daniel's God had performed. He went home where three times a day he prayed, kneeling on his knees; giving thanks to his God as he had been doing before. Daniel was persistent in his praying no matter what the king decreed; not hiding in his closet, but opening his windows so all could see. No matter what the opposition thought, Daniel was going to be found faithful before his God. I'm sure when Daniel started praying, he thought God would change the king's mind about the decree and Daniel wouldn't have to face the lions. When that didn't turn out to be the will of God for his life, he accepted whatever happened, even if it meant death. In doing so, God kept Daniel when he was thrown into the lion's den. In Daniel's persistent prayers to God, a witness of the faithfulness of our Father was written for all to see and believe.

We all come across difficulties and oppositions in our walk with God; but probably not as dire as being thrown in the lions' den. But sometimes in our eyes, they seem that bad. If we will remain persistent in seeking God's will in the matter, maybe our testimony will be a witness to others, much like Daniel's. Don't lose that enthusiasm for God by keeping your focus on the weeds. Instead, keep praising Him through every situation and difficulty. Get excited about what He is doing in your life and continually give Him praise in all things. Pray without ceasing. Let His name be forever on your lips.

We give Him all praise and all glory.

41

Light

Light – the natural agent that stimulates sight and makes things visible

Genesis 1:1-4(KJV) - In the beginning God created the heaven and the earth. And the earth was without form, and void; and darkness was upon the face of the deep. And the Spirit of God moved upon the face of the waters. And God said, Let there be light: and there was light. And God saw the light, that it was good; and God divided the light from the darkness.

At the beginning of time, there was nothing but formlessness and confusion. The Spirit of God moved into the mayhem and He said let there be light. He didn't speak darkness into existence. It was already there. No – He stepped into the darkness and the light of His countenance showed all about. God saw what the light did to the darkness and He was pleased. He saw His light separated night and day – darkness and light – evil and good – Satan and Jesus. He created day and night for our benefit; so that in the natural we can see what light does to darkness. When we walk in His Spirit, we realize that His Light will drive out the darkness in us and that should be our greatest desire. The apostle John wrote about how God is light.

I John 1:5-7(KJV) – This then is the message which we have heard of Him, and declare unto you, that God is light, and in Him is no darkness at all. If we say that we have fellowship with Him, and walk in darkness, we lie, and do not the truth: but if we walk in the light, as He is in the light, we have fellowship one with another, and the blood of Jesus Christ His Son cleanseth us from all sin.

In the first letter to the churches, John reminds the church that in the beginning was the Word, and the Word was with God, and the Word was God. John 1:4-5(KJV) in Him was life, and that life was the light of men. And the light shines in the darkness, and the darkness doesn't understand what the light is. John goes on to witness to them details he heard and things he had seen of that Light. He is relating all of this to them; so that they may remember the promises of Jesus that have manifested in their lives. He tells them that if we walk in the path God has for us; we are walking in His light, being filled with His countenance. But if we walk in darkness, continue down the path of ungodliness and immorality, and say we are a Christian, we are lying because we do not practice the truth. Many walk in the darkness of this world, not experiencing the light that God has for them. If we walk in this light, we are as a lightbulb to the world.

In the natural, we take the light that comes from lightbulbs for granted. We flip the light switch and suddenly the room is brighter. It is interesting how the lightbulb is much like our walk with God when His light shines through us. The lightbulb converts electric energy into light energy. It is made up of a positive and a negative terminal inside a glass casing, with a filament joining the two terminals. Once the power is supplied to the terminals, the electrical flow heats up the filament to the point that it begins to glow and light fills the void, overtaking the darkness. If the lightbulb stops working, it means the thin coil has snapped and therefore electricity can't make a complete circuit. This is much like God's light that shines through us. Our spirit is the earthly filament in this bodily lightbulb. God's Spirit flows into us much like the electric current, the positive God-filled energy flowing into our spirit and replacing the negative energy of our soul. Much as when the filament in the lightbulb is heated to glowing because the current passes through it, our spirit glows when the Spirit of God passes through us; causing our God-filled spirit to shine into the darkness. If our spirit doesn't shine, it is not because God isn't sending His Spirit into us. It is because our spirit is broken and doesn't make a complete connection; allowing Him to flow through us. We are called to walk with Jesus in the light. But many choose to walk in darkness; choosing not to bring out into His light all the evil in their hearts.

II Corinthians 4:3-4, 6(KJV) – But if our gospel be hid, it is hid to them that are lost: in whom the god of this world hath blinded the minds of them which believe not, lest the light of the glorious gospel of Christ, who is the image of God, should shine unto them. For God, who commanded the light to shine out of darkness, hath shined in our hearts to give the light of the knowledge of the glory of God in the face of Jesus Christ.

Paul is writing to the church at Corinth that there are those whose mind has been blinded by the enemy and they won't believe the gospel on their own. Satan, the god of this world, has made them unable to see the light of Jesus shining in those of us who are witnesses of His love. They can't seem to understand the light of the good news being preached to them. In Matthew 5, Jesus told us we are called to be the salt of the earth and the light of the world. Don't be a lightbulb that has a broken filament, but be one whose filament is found whole so the power of the Spirit of God may flow through you to reach others.

I know, you are asking yourself - how do I do that? The power of the Spirit of God doesn't just start flowing through you like the electrical current does through the wires. The Holy Spirit dwells within us when we spend time in the presence of God, whether in prayer or reading His word. Moses came down from the mountain, having spent 40 days and nights in the presence of God. He had fasted the whole time he was there. When he returned to the camp of the children of Israel, he didn't realize his face glowed and was radiant from being in the presence of God.

> Exodus 34:29-30(KJV) – And it came to pass, when Moses came down from mount Sinai with the two tables of testimony in Moses' hand, when he came down from the mount, that Moses wist not that the skin of his face shone while he talked with him. And when Aaron and all the children of Israel saw Moses', behold, the skin of his face shone; and they were afraid to come nigh him.

Moses had spent forty days and nights in the presence of the Father, conversing with Him, which caused his face to glow from being in the company of God. However, Moses didn't just start out his relationship with God during those forty days. He was called by God to bring the children of Israel out of Egypt forty years earlier. He then wandered in the desert for approximately 40 years before he was prepared to accomplish God's plan. I am sure that leaving the palace of the pharaoh and fleeing to Midian to herd sheep was a culture shock for him and he probably needed an attitude adjustment or two. During all those years, there were plenty of conversations between Moses and

God; preparing Moses for his time with the rebellious, complaining children of Israel. It took growing in the things of God to come to the place where he could see the glory of the Father as it passed by him. His face shone as a reflection of what he had seen of God. This same shine is something we should all aspire to in our Christian walk.

What happens when the light in the room goes out? Darkness consumes the void and takes its place. We are called to stand in a powerful stance and be a vessel the Holy Spirit can shine through for others to see. We need to let God's power shine through us, so that the world may see Jesus, the hope of glory.

> Isaiah 60:1-2(KJV) – Arise, shine; for thy light is come, and the glory of the Lord is risen upon thee. For, behold, the darkness shall cover the earth, and gross darkness the people: but the Lord shall arise upon thee, and His glory shall be seen upon thee.

We give Him all praise and all glory.

42

Season

Season – *a suitable, natural, or convenient time.*

After Jesus had risen from the dead, He met with His disciples, giving them final instructions before He was taken up and ascended into heaven.

Acts 1:7(KJV) – And He said unto them, It is not for you to know the times or the seasons, which the Father hath put in His own power.

This word 'season' in Greek means opportune time, the perfect timing of the Father. The disciples had been asking Jesus if this was the time when He would set up His kingdom on earth. Is this when He was going to rule and reign in the earthly realm? They were still looking for a king to take the nation of Israel back from the Romans. Jesus tells them it is not for them to know the timing of God; they couldn't understand it yet as they were still thinking with their carnal mind. He goes on to tell them in Acts 1:8(KJV) – But ye shall receive power, after that the Holy Ghost is come upon you. As they walk in that 'dunamis' power, that miraculous power that comes from being filled with the Holy Ghost, they would begin to understand God's timing and His purpose.

Understanding doesn't come all at once. It is line upon line, here a little and there a little, as you grow into the fullness of God. It takes time to grow into the calling and purpose God has for your life and with the 'dunamis' power that is given by the indwelling of the Holy Ghost with evidence of speaking in tongues, you are able to persist in that walk until you are filled completely with Him.

While Paul was in prison, he wrote to his protégé, Timothy, giving him instructions for passing along the faith to the next generation.

> II Timothy 4:2-4(KJV) – Preach the word; be instant in season, out of season; reprove, rebuke, exhort with all long-suffering and doctrine. For the time will come when they will not endure sound doctrine; but after their own lusts shall they heap to themselves teachers, having itching ears; and they shall turn away their ears from the truth, and shall be turned unto fables.

In these scriptures, the word season has two different meanings. The first 'season' means when it is a convenient opportunity, when it is favorable or appropriate. The second 'season' means when the opportunity is not convenient, when the timing doesn't seem right and you are not sure how the word will be received. But it is not yours to know the times or the seasons. Paul is telling Timothy that no matter the circumstance, proclaim openly the gospel of Jesus Christ, as hard times will come. People will not listen to the truth that comes from the pure Word of God. They will be more interested in words that make them feel good about the choices they have made. They will look for teachers who will tell them what they want to hear. So be ready, in a precise moment of time, to speak the word that the Holy Spirit speaks to you. We need to be sensitive to the moving of the Holy Spirit in our lives, so we are ready to speak His word, no matter if it makes sense to you or not. This past week, I was out doing some shopping and when I finished, I went up to the checkout. As I approached the cashier, the Holy Spirit spoke into my spirit words He would have me say to her. He told me to tell her "You have a beautiful complexion". These were not words that I would normally say to someone, but I was obedient and spoke the words. Her reply was, "Thank you very much for telling me that. I needed to hear it." She then went on to tell me thoughts she was having about herself that were tearing her down, thoughts meant to make her think less of herself. It was the perfect timing of the Lord to build her up. We can never know what is in the heart of another person. Only God knows the season to speak into someone's life. How many of you have a jacket with a hood attached or a hoodie sweatshirt? God showed me that to be instant in season is much like having a jacket with a hood. For me, the hood always seems to be in the way behind my head. When it's mild outside and the wind is not blowing, the hood is inconvenient, as I don't need it right then. But I need the jacket, so I have to take the hood along with the jacket. But when it gets really cold outside, and the wind is blowing, the hood, though it has not been convenient, is needful to keep me warm. You bring the hood along, whether it is useful or not; just as we are to be ready with the Word of God, whether it is an opportune time, or it doesn't feel like the best time to deliver the word. We are to be the official messenger bringing the word of God, whether we feel like it is the best time. There will be times when the Holy Ghost gives you a word for someone and it is received with joy. Then there will be those times when you know that the word will not be received; but by the prompting of the Holy Ghost, you give the word anyway.

Isaiah 50:4(KJV) – The Lord God hath given me the tongue of the learned, that I should know how to speak a word in season to him that is weary: He wakeneth morning by morning, He wakeneth mine ear to hear as the learned.

God has equipped all of those who are His for the calling He has for them. And not until the Holy Ghost indwells in us do we begin to understand His calling and His timing. We should wake each morning with the desire to hear His word in our ears, to listen to His voice of instruction. Too many times the Holy Spirit prompts us to speak a word to someone and we feel we know better than Him on what to speak. It is not our position to question the timing or the word of the Lord. The God we serve created all things that you can see and things you can't see. He knows everything, inside and out. So why would we want to hold back on a word He has given us and not want to walk into the full purpose He has for our life? God's timing is always perfect. God is never late, never early, but always on time. Our season is not always God's season. But there are two benefits in operating in God's season. It increases your faith, as you are forced to trust that the words you have received are from God and that it is His perfect timing. Plus, it makes certain that He, and only He, gets the glory and praise for bringing us through. In our walk with God, our desire should be to wait on His perfect timing, His season for every area of our life. If we allow Jesus to order our steps, we will always be in His season.

Proverbs 15:23(KJV) – A man hath joy by the answer of his mouth: and a word spoken in due season, how good is it!

We give Him all praise and all glory.

43

Feed

Feed – *an act of giving food, especially to animals or a baby,*
or of having food given to one.

During the second year of His ministry on earth, Jesus heard that John the Baptist had been beheaded by Herod. John was the one called to prepare the way for Jesus but he was also related to Jesus through His mother Mary. I am sure Jesus was moved by this loss, so He took His disciples with Him to a deserted place near Bethsaida. By now, the news of His miracles and healings had reached multitudes and they followed Him out of the nearby towns to where He was camped. Bethsaida must have been in a populated area as there were five thousand men plus women and children gathered to hear Jesus that day. He felt compassion for them as they hadn't walked to the nearby synagogue to hear Him, but most likely traveled up to five, maybe even ten, miles to get where He was.

John 6:5(KJV) – When Jesus then lifted up His eyes, and saw a great company come unto Him, He saith unto Philip, Whence shall we buy bread, that these may eat?

Jesus already knew the answer to this question, but it was a test for the disciples to teach them a lesson in miracles. How many times does God use a test in your life to teach you a lesson? Philip's logical answer to the question was, 'Master, it would take six months' wages to buy enough for all of them to have just a morsel.' The disciple Andrew piped up, telling Jesus that a boy was in the group who had five loaves and two fishes, but how is that small lunch going to feed all these people? Andrew was also looking at the situation from a logical standpoint. They were both looking at the natural, how much money it would take, or how many people needed to be fed. Mutually Philip and Andrew were limiting the way to deal with this situation. They had taken their eyes off Jesus and put them on the circumstances.

John 6:10(KJV) – And Jesus said, Make the men sit down. Now there was much grass in the place. So, the men sat down, in number about five thousand.

There are three things John is pointing out in this scripture. Jesus told the men to sit down, which means they were probably all standing up. In Mark 6:34-35(KJV) it says – 'And Jesus, when He came out, saw much people, and was moved with compassion toward them, because they were as sheep not having a shepherd: and He began to teach them many things. And when the day was now far spent, His disciples came unto Him, reminding Him that they were in a desert place and time has passed for a meal.' I'm sure there wasn't a food court anywhere near or a taco truck waiting down the hill. The multitude had walked all the way to follow Jesus and then had been standing all the time He was teaching. With them all standing, they wouldn't have been able to see how Jesus would accomplish the miracle of feeding all of them. Jesus wanted them to be in a position of rest, so He had them sit. Also, in this scripture, we are told the area was covered in grass pastures, reminding us that Psalm 23:2(KJV) tells us – He maketh me to lie down in green pastures. He put them in a comfortable position to enjoy the meal that Jesus would provide for them. This wouldn't be a snack and then head back home, Jesus was going to feed them until they were full in the natural; as He had just done in His spiritual teaching to them. The third point this scripture makes is that there were five thousand men in attendance; which does not include women or children. Jesus instructed the disciples to have all the people sit in groups of fifty. This showed to both the disciples and the assembly the significance of the miracle that was about to be done. His disciples were so touched that the account was written in all four gospels in the New Testament.

John 6:11(KJV) – And Jesus took the loaves; and when He had given thanks, He distributed to the disciples, and the disciples to them that were set down; and likewise of the fishes as much as they would.

Jesus didn't just bless the loaves and fishes and suddenly there was a buffet with enough food to feed all the people; He didn't magically make enough food all at once. Jesus took the five loaves and two fishes (all that was available), He blessed them and then began to break them into pieces. The scripture doesn't say it, but I think that each disciple took his turn loading up with all he could carry of bread and fish before heading to feed a section of fifty in the multitude. I am sure the disciples were thinking that they could never feed five thousand with five loaves and two fishes. After the first section was fed, they probably were walking back to Jesus thinking, 'What am I going to do when I get up there and there is no more food? How will I be able to face the next group without anything to feed them?' The more groups they fed, the greater their faith began to grow. The original five loaves and two fishes never ran out until all five thousand men plus the women and children had been fed and the leftovers were gathered in twelve baskets. This is an excellent example of not limiting the Holy One of Israel; don't look at your situation and say 'I only'. If we offer our bread and fish to Him, He will fill us until we are full to overflowing. Whatever we are lacking, whether it be finances, time, patience or anything we are short on, if we will lay the portion we have at Jesus' feet, He will take it, bless it, and provide what we need until we are full.

John 6:35(KJV) – And Jesus said unto them, I am the bread of life; he that cometh to me shall never hunger; and he that believeth on Me shall never thirst.

Jesus is the Bread of Life. He feeds you in bits, in pieces; it is line upon line, here a little, there a little. He doesn't show us the end, the completeness of what He has planned for our lives. He just gives us a morsel, a taste of what is to come. Just as we can't see what is going on inside our body, under our skin, but must believe that it is functioning; we can't see the outcome that God has for our lives, but we know He is working on our behalf. So, if we keep our eyes on Jesus, He will keep us fed to the point of always being full. At the times you feel like you don't have much in your life, give it to Jesus; He can multiply it for His use. We are called to be the bread that He uses to feed a dying world, giving them the Bread of Life that is Jesus Christ. So, desire the pure bread in your life, so that you may feed it to others.

We give Him all praise and all glory.

44

Anxiety

Anxiety – *a feeling of worry, nervousness, or unease, typically about an imminent event with an uncertain outcome.*

We don't realize how much control our mind has over us; that part of us that would like to perceive and understand by feeling, judging, and determining. The mind always wants to know the outcome of an event before it even happens; so it can be prepared for whatever is about to occur. How are we walking in the faith of God in that? If you allow your mind to start to ponder on upcoming circumstances and situations, you are planting a seed of concern and fretfulness to begin to take root. If you let it into your spirit, you have already let it win. In our carnal mind, which is our thought process, by the time you let anxiety in, you have let worry in, and then doubt and unbelief won't be far behind. The best place to beat it is before it begins. It is in the mind, the thought realm, that the spirit of anxiousness and worry comes over us. But we aren't called to walk by sight, will, or emotion of our own desires; we are called to walk by faith in the will of God.

Ephesians 4:17(KJV) – This I say therefore, and testify in the Lord, that ye henceforth walk not as other Gentiles walk, in the vanity of their mind.

In this scripture, Paul wrote to the church at Ephesus, that we are to grow up in every way into Christ Jesus. This entails not walking as the world walks, with their mind ruled by earthly emotions. He tells us to put off our old man, the former way of life, that caused anxiety and worry. Instead, we should be ready to put on our new self, one that has allowed God to renew our attitude and spirit; walking in His peace. It is in the renewing of our mind that we are transformed, that our carnal mind is changed to be more like Jesus. We can't renew our minds on our own. All of our help comes from God. He is our source in every season of our lives. We should be asking ourselves; 'Do I have the mind of Christ in this situation?'

Romans 12:2(KJV) – And be not conformed to this world: but be ye transformed by the renewing of your mind, that ye may prove what is that good, and acceptable, and perfect, will of God.

The enemy would like to mold you into the image of the world, the rat race that comes from trying to make things happen, no matter the cost. You work at a job that consumes your mind all day; and you go home to a house that needs your attention evenings and weekends, to sit down in front of the television to watch mindless programs with commercials that plant seeds of worry and anxiety. Then you go off to bed; only to find your mind wandering into areas of 'What if'; which feeds the anxiety and worry. Paul is telling the church at Ephesus, that they are not to live as before, wrapping themselves in the world and its bankrupt values. We are to allow the Holy Spirit to change us into another form, a transformation of our mind for the better from the inside out. When you have allowed the enemy to plant worry and anxiety in your mind, you have lost the peace of God. You have taken over your life and not placed yourself in God's care. The only way to transform your mind is to renew it in the Word of God.

> Philippians 4:8(KJV) – Finally, brethren, whatsoever things are true, whatsoever things are honest, whatsoever things are just, whatsoever things are pure, whatsoever things are lovely, whatsoever things are of good report; if there be any virtue, and if there be any praise, think on these things.

If you look at this list, there is nothing on it that would cause anxiety or worry. Everything on this list brings the peace of God into your spirit; the peace that passes all understanding. So, if whatever thought that is causing you anxiety is not on this list, then quit thinking about it. Instead, pray. Pray for everything; God enjoys hearing from each of us. So, talk to Him about your needs and be thankful for what has come. Pray in the Spirit, shutting down your mind. Speak the Word of God into your life by reading His word out loud. Fill your thought process with words of praise and virtue. And know that the peace of God that passes all understanding will fill your heart and mind.

There is nothing that will happen to us that God doesn't already know. He is still in control of everything. This is why Jesus taught in Matthew– Take no thought for tomorrow. We should be taking prisoners of every thought, every emotion; and subduing them into the obedience of God. Every worry, fret, or anxious feeling begins with our mind, creating a thought that sets itself up against the true knowledge of God. How can you expect to receive strength from God if you just let any thought in? How can you expect peace in your life if you don't control your thoughts? You have the authority over what is allowed into your mind. You have control of your mind, will, and emotions. II Corinthians 10 tells us we are to bring into captivity every thought, and every emotion to the obedience of Christ. Do not allow the anxiety to consume you. It is your decision to walk in God's peace or allow the enemy to fill your mind with thoughts of anxiety, worry, and fear.

When I was growing up, I was a chronic worrier. I worried about everything. By the time I was in the third grade I had a stomach ulcer. It wasn't until I was married that I began to address the doubt in me that caused the anxiety and unease in my thoughts. I learned that worrying didn't change the situation at all. As Jesus taught – Matthew 6:27(KJV)Which of you by taking thought can add one cubit unto his stature? The anxiety and anxiousness caused me to worry more. It wasn't until I was filled with the Holy Ghost with evidence of speaking in tongues that I took control of my mind. By the prompting of the Holy Spirit, I collected scriptures to recite when worry began to take over my mind. Such as Psalm 34:7(KJV) – The angel of the Lord encampeth round about them that fear Him and delivereth them. I began to realize that there was nothing I needed to fear because Jesus goes before me in all situations. Or Psalm 18:32(KJV) – It is God that girdeth me with strength, and maketh my way perfect. He makes my path straight and gives me the power to walk every situation out. I have learned that my source is God and there is nothing else I need. It is important that each of us have our weapons of the word of God to defeat the enemy in our thoughts and that we use them. In the last two years we have seen the world as we know it change drastically. However, this is only the beginning of things to come. It is very important that we learn how to discern between the whispers of Satan and the voice of God. Satan will only cause anxiety, worry, unease, and fear; where the voice of God brings peace. This discernment will be the saving grace to those who are the sons of God, because we will not be moved by external circumstances. Get before the Father and seek His guidance in developing the peace that the world cannot give.

We give Him all praise and all glory.

45

Enough

Enough – *as much or as many as required, sufficient, adequate*

If you were stranded on a deserted island, what would the one thing you would want to have with you? Would you want a box of matches to start a fire that would keep you warm when the nights got cold and so you would be able to cook? How about a fishing net to catch the food you are going to cook? Or maybe even a knife to clean the fish and cut limbs to put in the fire? It would really be difficult to narrow it down to just one item that would be enough to help you make it through your isolation on the island. If you picked the matches, how would you clean your catch and get kindling to start the fire? If it was the knife you chose, how would you start the fire to cook the fish that you had to catch with your hands because you didn't have a net? How about someone to come alongside on the island, so you don't have to be self-sufficient? We are given that through God.

II Corinthians 12:9-10(KJV) – And He said unto me, My grace is sufficient for thee: for my strength is made perfect in weakness. Most gladly therefore will I rather glory in my infirmities, that the power of Christ may rest upon me. Therefore, I take pleasure in infirmities, in reproaches, in necessities, in persecutions, in distresses for Christ's sake: for when I am weak, then I am strong.

In this letter, Paul is writing to the church at Corinth concerning the claims made by false teachers. They were trying to discredit him before the Corinthian church, stating that he was inferior to the real ministers. He writes that we are not sufficient in ourselves to think anything comes from us, but our sufficiency is of God. None of us are adequately qualified in ourselves alone to claim that anything originates from us, but it all comes from the almighty God who gives freely to those who ask. Paul goes on to tell them about his struggle with a thorn in the flesh and how he prayed to God three times to remove it. The answer from God to his prayer was II Corinthians 12:9(KJV)- My lovingkindness and My mercy are all you need. In your weakness My power in you is made strong. Paul says he would rather gladly recognize his inferiorities, his frailty in the flesh, even the persecutions for Jesus' sake because when he is weak in himself, he is strong in Jesus. Even the great apostle Paul had to be reminded that the grace of God is enough; He is all Paul needed to make it through all the trials, battles, and criticism that came his way. Whenever we recognize our weakness, then the great I AM can step in and be strong in our life. We will never be enough in and of ourself.

In the Old Testament, Belshazzar, the son of the king of Babylon, held a state dinner, inviting his officials, along with his wives and concubines to join him. He ordered the servants to bring in the gold and silver vessels that had been stolen from the temple in Jerusalem many years earlier. When the vessels were delivered, the invited guests drank wine. Daniel 5:4(KJV) – They drank wine, and praised the gods of gold, and of silver, of brass, of iron, of wood, and of stone. Then the finger of a man's hand appeared in the banquet hall and wrote a phrase in the plaster on the wall. Belshazzar could not interpret what was written, so after several attempts by court astrologers, Daniel was called upon to interpret the words. Daniel told Belshazzar that he had been weighed on God's scales of righteousness and found inadequate. Belshazzar lacked the grace and mercy of God and of himself. He was not enough. I am sure this was hard for a regent to hear as he ruled a mighty, powerful nation. Instead of praising the God of righteousness at his banquet, Belshazzar and his guests praised the gods of power, status, strength, abundance, and wisdom. The writing from God is telling him that he is not the top dog he thought he was. Daniel also tells him that Belshazzar' days as king are coming to an end and his precious kingdom would be divided and given to others. That night, Belshazzar was murdered in his sleep. The difference between Paul and Belshazzar is that when Belshazzar thought he was strong, he was truly weak.

In writing each week's bible study, by Monday I usually have received the specific word from God for me to write about; but this week there had been silence. I have been writing these studies long enough to know when it is God that is speaking to and through me or when I am writing out of myself. So yesterday, I started studying in Leviticus about the feasts the children of Israel celebrated. I spent most of the day reading and waiting for the Holy Spirit to move through the scriptures, but nothing happened. Then, when prayer time came, I got down on my face and prayed, pleading with God to reveal why I hadn't received His word yet. He reminded me that I hadn't asked for His word. I had been working on a word, studying out a word; but not the word He chose. I was trying to do it in and of myself; not allowing Him to be all that was required to get His calling in my life accomplished. Then when I was in the shower this morning, Tuesday, He dropped this week's word into my spirit. He reminded me if I would just ask Him,

He would be enough for me in every situation. He would walk with me through every trial and temptation. He would provide all my needs according to His riches in glory. He would lead me down the path He has for me, telling me when to turn to the right or to the left. I would find His strength in my weakness.

We all have a reason to be here, a mission that God knew before the creation of the earth. We should each purpose to know that He is all we need in our life to make our calling sure, He is enough. II Peter 1:9(KJV) tells us -Wherefore the rather, brethren, give diligence to make your calling and election sure: for if ye do these things, ye shall never fall. Lock in on your calling, on what God has called you to do. He knew there would be a thorn in your flesh, there would be something in you that would remind you that of your own you are not enough. But in Him, there is not anything He can't accomplish in you. Don't let others try to tell you that you are missing out on things in life when you make God enough. And don't allow the world to draw you into the lust of the flesh, always wanting more. We all live with this anxiety for more, more, more. It is a prison that obsesses us. The world taunts us that bigger is always better, newer is the best and you need it all. But all we need is Jesus in our life, the Holy Spirit moving in our lives to be exactly what He has called us to be. Be content in Jesus, knowing that He will do all in your life. Be content in where He has placed you. We are to fulfill the life He has purposed for us. What is the one thing that you have chosen to help you make it through your walk on this earth? Are you secure enough in your walk with Jesus to allow Him to be enough for you?

We give Him all praise and all glory.

46

Commitment

Commitment – an agreement or pledge to do something in the future.

How many of you made resolutions at the beginning of the year? You committed to yourself that this was the year you were going to do it, you were going to accomplish your pledge. Maybe it was to exercise more and lose those few extra pounds. Or it was to curb your spending with the ultimate goal of getting out of debt. And how long did those lofty pledges last you? Did you even make it to Valentine's Day before you decided you could miss a day? Then one time leads to another and soon your resolutions are just a memory of another year failed at your commitment. How about that target to read the Bible and pray every day? If the resolutions we make, and the goals that we set for our life are not in our hearts, they will never be accomplished. We think it would be a good idea to read the Bible and we pray whenever we need something or we are in trouble. But do we have the perseverance to keep at it long enough for it to become a habit? If it is a commitment worth the life-changing effect, it is worth blocking out time to achieve it and sticking to it. How strong is your determination?

Psalm 37:5(KJV) – Commit thy way unto the Lord; trust also in Him; and He shall bring it to pass.

In Hebrew, the word 'commit' means to roll off onto. If we will roll the direction of our life to God, putting all our confidence in Him that He will accomplish it, He will make it happen. We don't commit because then we would have to give up control in our lives. You pray each day to learn the direction God has for you, to hear His voice saying go to the right or to the left. You read the Bible, allowing Him to speak to you through His Word. The desire of your heart should be to become more like God, having more of Him in your life, longing for His presence in you. To make a commitment to last, you must realize that it is not going to happen in a day or two. Commitment comes from continuing in your actions even when you don't feel like it or there is something else that seems more important at the time; turning it all over to God and allowing Him to fulfill the resolution.

I prayed this week that God would show me an example of commitment in the Bible and He took me to the account of Ruth and Naomi.

Ruth 1:16-17(KJV) – And Ruth said, Entreat me not to leave thee, or to return from following after thee: for whither thou goest, I will go; and where thou lodgest, I will lodge: thy people shall be my people, and thy God my God: Where thou diest, will I die, and there will I be buried: the Lord do so to me, and more also, if ought but death part thee and me.

In the book of Ruth, we read of Naomi and her husband leaving Bethlehem because of the famine and relocating to Moab. While there, both of the sons married women of Moab. Then, in time, Naomi's husband and her sons died. This left Naomi and her two daughters-in-law as widows. With no relatives in Moab, Naomi decided to go back to Bethlehem; at least there she would have kinsmen who would help take care of her. After much discussion and tears, it was decided that one daughter-in-law would go back to her people, but Ruth was going with Naomi to Bethlehem. The deciding factor was Ruth's measure of commitment to Naomi who we just read in scripture. Moab was not a God-fearing nation, but a pagan nation. I am sure Ruth grew up not hearing a word about Jehovah, but during her time with Naomi, there had been a witness go forth from the older Jewish lady. There was something in Naomi's life that Ruth could see and she wanted it. It was Naomi's commitment unto her God that led Ruth's pledge to live her life with Naomi, even until death, and her vow to follow Naomi's God. This pledge, this commitment of Ruth's to Naomi, put a Moabite woman in the lineage of Jesus Christ.

Let's look at the chicken and the pig. They both contribute to your breakfast. The chicken provides the egg for your scrambled eggs and the pig supplies the ham to complement your eggs. The only difference is that the chicken just provided something. The pig committed his whole life to supply for your breakfast. The pig doesn't really have a choice, he just has to live up to his commitment. Are you in relationships that you just contribute to occasionally, just when it is convenient? Instead, are you committed to the relationship, dropping everything when needed and giving of yourself? The value of commitment has waned over the years making it easy to give up on something that requires extra effort, sacrifice of time or even oneself. Marriage is the best example of commitment in a relationship on earth. But, in modern day society, people favor living together over making a pledge to someone that includes until death do us part. Without the commitment, each party has the ability to end the relationship whenever it is convenient, instead of working through the trials that come up. Making a commitment means making a sacrifice; putting something or someone before you. If you can't make a commitment to other people, how can you ever make a commitment to God?

Do you realize the commitment Jesus made for each of us? He gave His life that we may live! In Matthew 28:20b(KJV), Jesus tells us – I am with you always, even unto the end of the world. The word world in this scripture means forever, His commitment is that He will be with you forever, eternally. He doesn't expect more from us than He is willing to give of Himself.

Paul gave us a good example of commitment to what God can do with our life if we commit it all unto Him. II Timothy 4:7(KJV) says 'I have fought a good fight, I have finished my course, I have kept the faith.' We each have been given a course, a race to run in Jesus Christ and are not in the same place in our individual races. As Paul writes, there is a fight in this race. The enemy doesn't want you to finish and will do whatever it takes to get you to abandon the course and cause you to lose interest in finishing. Paul reminds Timothy that it takes faith, the conviction that God is in control and will be with you every step of the way. How many of you are just contributing in your race with Jesus? Are you here to just give an egg every once in a while, just when it is convenient for you? The condition of our nation is changing constantly and not for the better. We have become a country of uncommitted people, who are only concerned about themselves. We have forgotten what it meant to pledge our allegiance to our country. When the going gets tough here, when the enemy comes to silence you for claiming Jesus is Lord, will you stick around? Do you have the commitment it takes to keep up the fight until the race is won? Don't lose your hope in Jesus Christ. Get in the place that you know, that you know, that you are where God planted you and STAY THERE!! Then begin to let Him use you and STAY AT IT!! Commitment takes time and faithfulness, line upon line, here a little and there a little. Ephesians 2:10(KJV) says that we are His workmanship, created in Christ Jesus unto good works, which God hath before ordained that we should walk in them. Don't just contribute to your walk; commit to being faithful in each step taken, so you can say I have fought a good fight, finished my course and kept the faith.

We give Him all praise and all glory.

47

Cup

Cup – *a small bowl-shaped container for drinking from, typically having a handle.*

Acts 3:1-8(KJV) – Now Peter and John went up together into the temple at the hour of prayer, being the ninth hour. And a certain man lame from his mother's womb was carried, whom they laid daily at the gate of the temple which is called Beautiful, to ask alms of them that entered into the temple; Who seeing Peter and John about to go into the temple asked an alms. And Peter, fastening his eyes upon him with John, said, Look on us. And he gave heed unto them, expecting to receive something of them. Then Peter said, Silver and gold have I none; but such as I have give I thee: In the name of Jesus Christ of Nazareth rise up and walk. And he took him by the right hand, and lifted him up: and immediately his feet and ankle bones received strength. And he leaping up stood, and walked, and entered with them into the temple, walking, and leaping, and praising God.

Peter and John were on their way to the temple for prayer at about three o'clock in the afternoon. This was one of the designated public times for daily prayer and was an opportune time for the disadvantaged to beg for money. A certain man who could not walk since he was born was carried by someone every day to the temple gate called Beautiful. This gate was most likely on the outside of the temple, as no one with an issue of any kind was allowed into the temple. Consequently, this man sat on his pallet every day asking for a gift from those who would be most likely to give. If this were a present-day scene, the man would have had a cup in his hand to collect the money. I can see him saying, "Alms for the poor, does anyone have alms for the poor?"; holding out his cup to gather what was given to him. It didn't take much faith to ask for a compassionate act from those entering into the temple. He was just looking for a couple of alms to buy his lunch for that day, but God had more planned than that. When Peter and John walked by, he asked for a compassionate donation. Peter looked intently at him and said, Look at us; causing a sense of expectation to rise up in the man; thinking maybe these men will give me some money. Peter wanted the man to see that it wasn't money or anything tangible that he was getting. Peter told him that he didn't have any silver or gold, but what he did have, he would give to him. Peter was confident in the name of Jesus, which represents authority and power to those who are filled with the Holy Ghost. Peter told him, in the name of Jesus Christ, get up and walk. Then Peter took him by his right hand. You know when you reach out to help someone get up, you offer them your right hand and they take it with their right hand. In the Bible, the right hand represents power; Peter was offering the lame man the power of God for his life. The man's ankle and feet bones were instantly strengthened and made firm and he was filled with joy; praising God.

Now let's take a look at the cup; whether it be literal as with the lame man or figurative as with Jesus in the garden. We all have a cup that we hold out to God, a vessel to receive what God provides us. In our prayers, we have been asking; even pleading; with God to supply what we think we need. We know exactly what we have decided in our own mind will take care of our deficiency; we know what we would like to see in our cup. How many of you have looked in your cup and found the answer God supplied for you was not what you felt you needed? Or maybe you even rejected what God placed in your cup. The lame man at the gate never imagined he would receive anything more than maybe a few alms. But God had in mind a greater provision than anything the man could have expected. He doesn't meet your expectations because He exceeds it. And His supplies aren't necessarily just monetary. If we just ask Him, He will fill up our spiritual, mental, emotional, and physical reserves. In other words, He will recharge our battery. But it probably won't be in the way you expected. King David wrote about his cup.

Psalm 23:5(KJV) – Thou preparest a table before me in the presence of mine enemies: thou anointest my head with oil; my cup runneth over.

David realizes that God will not stop the enemies from coming after the king, but the Father will put him in situations where he is confronted with those adversaries. Not only will God put him in the presence of his enemies, but David will sit down at the king's table with those opponents. But the Almighty Father would anoint David's head with oil, showing God's favor and blessings, and then He filled David's cup until it was running over with His mercy. At this table, David was able to drink of the Father's favor and mercy. If you had been David, what would your reaction have been? Are you able to sit where God places your cup, confident in His favor and mercy?

Psalm 16:5(KJV) -The Lord is the portion of mine inheritance and of my cup: Thou maintainest my lot.

God is my sustenance and my life-giving cup. In that cup, Father, You hold my future and my eternal riches. We must believe that God is all we need and He will supply all of our needs according to His riches in glory by Christ Jesus.

How many times have you dismissed something in your cup when it didn't match what you thought you needed? You had this preconceived idea of exactly what you needed, but that is not what shows up. Last week I was sewing on a project and began to ponder on the age of my twenty seven year old sewing machine and how much longer it would last. I knew that the purchase of a new one was not in my budget at the time, so I put that thought aside and concentrated on my sewing. Later that day I received a text from someone that wanted me to do a small sewing project for them. Along with the request for sewing, she wrote that she had a sewing machine that was her grandmother's and would I like to have it. Originally, I thought I would get a new one, with all the updated conveniences on it; but God had another plan. I realized that He was placing the sewing machine that I needed in my cup and I had the choice whether to receive the blessing or deny the provision that God was making for my life. We are all given the option of taking what God places in our cup or rejecting it. We can go with the preconceived idea that we know better what we need than our Heavenly Father does. Or we can make God our choice. Can you walk in the faith that His thoughts are not your thoughts, nor your ways His ways? Romans tells us the gifts and calling of God are without repentance, we won't regret choosing them. Will you take the right hand of God that He is offering or will you hold on to your empty cup? Learn the lesson of the lame man and allow God to fill your cup with the miracles He has for your life.

We give Him all praise and all glory.

48

Planted

Planted – placed in the ground so that it can grow, placed in a specified position.

> I Corinthians 12:12-14, 18(KJV) – For as the body is one, and hath many members, and all the members of that one body, being many, are one body: so also is Christ. For by one Spirit are we all baptized into one body, whether we be Jews or Gentiles, whether we be bond or free; and have been all made to drink into one Spirit, for the body is not one member, but many. But now hath God set the members every one of them in the body, as it hath pleased Him.

We are all to be part of the body of Christ; each of us growing up into Him. But how can we grow if we are not planted in the place God has chosen for us? Paul is using the example of the human body to teach how the body of Christ is made; just as our natural body is made up of many parts, so it is with the body God is calling each of us to be a part. It doesn't matter our nationality, our station in life, but we have all been made to be strengthened by one Holy Spirit. So, if we are all part of His Body, isn't it important for us to be where He has planted us, where He has placed us in His Body. My prayer is: "God, place me in the body as You see fit, a place where I can minister to and be ministered unto, where I can be the living vessel You would have me be." Nature gives us a very good example of being planted in the place that you are meant to be. My sister and I have tried our hand at gardening the last two years. We have learned that when you plant bell peppers in the hot Texas sun, they don't make it through July. But the okra plants just love the sweltering heat that the summers here bring. Romans 12:4(KJV) For as we are many members in one body, and all members have not the same office. Just like the bell peppers, some are called to bear the colorful fruit for which the plant is known; which is much like the praise and worship that comes forth to the Father. Then there are those who are called to be the okra plants, growing ever taller in the Light of the Son of God, standing straight as a standard and example for all to see. The body of Christ has many members and these are just two of the vast number of parts the Father has planned. Just like the bell peppers and the okra, if you are not planted in the place where God planned for you, you will bear little or no fruit. It takes all the plants in their God assigned place to complete the garden, just like it takes all the members of the Body of Christ in their assigned place to complete His plans. We are not called just to exist where God has planted us, just like the vegetables in the garden, we are placed there to produce fruit.

Jeremiah 29:4-7(KJV) – Thus saith the Lord of hosts, the God of Israel, unto all that are carried away captives, whom I have caused to be carried away from Jerusalem unto Babylon; build ye houses, and dwell in them; and plant gardens, and eat the fruit of them; take ye wives, and beget sons and daughters; and take wives for your sons, and give your daughters to husbands, that they may bear sons and daughters; that ye may be increased there, and not diminished. And seek the peace of the city whither I have caused you to be carried away captives, and pray unto the Lord for it: for in the peace thereof shall ye have peace.

Jeremiah is giving the exiles who King Nebuchadnezzar took from Jerusalem to Babylon instructions on how to live where the Lord has them for a season. The prophet wrote a letter to the elders, priests, prophets and all the rest who had been taken captive by the King. The order from the Lord was to build houses and dwell in them or for you and I, we are to dwell in the place where God has planted us all the days of our lives, allowing our roots to grow deep. The next instruction was to plant gardens and eat the fruit of them. First, we are to plant seeds, which is the word of God, into those we encounter; allowing them to be watered and the increase is given by God. A plant in the natural garden that does not bear fruit is not fit for the garden and is plucked up. So it is in the Spirit, if we do not bear fruit John 15 tells us Jesus will prune us. God then told the exiles to take wives and have children causing them to be further rooted in the place of banishment. Not only did He tell them to have sons and daughters, but also to have grandchildren. Families bring about stability, giving the place inhabited the feeling of home. In our place in the body of Christ, we are to live where we have been planted, making it our habitation; allowing us to flourish in God. Jeremiah prophesied the words of the Lord that not only are they to stay where they are right now, but they are to build houses, plant gardens and have families. God doesn't stop there with His instructions; He tells them to pray for the peace of their enemies, those people they hated. He promised that in praying for the peace of their captors, they will also find peace themselves. If we are planted where we should be in God, we will walk in peace. I Timothy 2 tells us to pray for those in authority over us, even if we don't agree with them, especially if we don't agree with them with the promise of I Timothy

2:2(KJV) - that we may lead a quiet and peaceable life in all Godliness and honesty. The children of Israel were restless in exile and wanted to revolt against King Nebuchadnezzar. Many of us are restless where God has planted us, there are those around us that don't believe the way we do, they don't have the same standards. Just like the children of Israel we want to rebel against God's will in our lives and move to some place where it is more comfortable, some place where you won't be stretched. We must all strive to abide in the place God has for us, in doing so, we can walk in His peace in our lives. If you are in someone else's place in the garden, you won't accomplish God's will for your life. Jeremiah 29:11(KJV) - For I know the thoughts that I think toward you, saith the Lord, thoughts of peace, and not of evil, to give you an expected end.

God will always accomplish His purpose. God's plan will come forth, it's not whether He will do it, but will He do it through you. In Genesis 1 when God spoke the lights in the firmament into existence, He made the sun for day and the moon for night. Now the moon never said, I don't want to be in the night, I want to be in the day. Instead, the moon said, 'Yes, Sir' and has been in his place of service since the beginning of time. The place where God plants you may be the most uncomfortable place you could imagine. Most times the thing you are most insecure about is the place where God has planted you. God knew everything about where He placed you even before you came into existence. When He spoke the birds in the air and the fish in the sea, they took their place. When God spoke your name, He had a specific place for you in His plan.

Philippians 2:13(KJV) – For it is God which worketh in you both to will and to do of His good pleasure.

199

God is working in each of our heart's, that we may desire and do His will in our lives. No matter where He has planted you, He has gone before you and provided all you will need to accomplish His work. Where He has planted you, He will feed you. His desire is that you know the work that He has for your life and that you let nothing interfere with it. Find your place in the body of Christ, do your part where you are planted, allow your roots to grow deep, bring forth the fruit of the Spirit and pray for the peace of God that passes all understanding to come upon those around you.

We give Him all praise and all glory.

49

Name

Name – *a word or set of words by which a person, animal, place, or thing is known, addressed, or referred to.*

At birth, each of us receives a name that will be carried with us all through our lives. There are some circumstances where that name is changed, but for the most part, we retain our birth names. At an early age, we all begin to introduce ourselves by this given name, saying 'I am Debbie' or whatever the name of the child is. The more you introduce yourself and the more others call you by this title, the more you realize this name defines 'you'. The Bible tells us we are not just identified by this given name; but also by the name that God has given us. Proverbs 22:1(KJV) – A good name is rather to be chosen than great riches. God has a good name that He calls each of us. There are several accounts in the bible where the given name was changed by God.

Genesis 12 tells us of the account of God calling Abram at the age of seventy-five. God appeared to him, giving him a word to move all his household to the land that God would show him.

Genesis 12:2(KJV) – And I will make of thee a great nation, and
I will bless thee, and make thy name great; and thou shalt be
a blessing:

God is telling Abram that from his descendants, God would cause a
great mass of people to be brought forth. Now this was going to be
quite a feat as Sarai, Abram's wife, was barren at the age of sixty-five.
A few years later, God appears to Abram and reminds him of the words
the Lord spoke back in Haran. Abram tells God that Sarai is still barren
and the only descendant he will have is a servant in his household; he
is still not sure how God is going to accomplish it. God shows Abram
that not only will his descendants form a great nation, but it will be so
large that just like the stars in the sky, they will be innumerable. Now
this is a huge promise from God, and in the carnal mind, Abram sees
no way it can happen. Even Sarai is getting a little frustrated, so she
offers her handmaid, Hagar, to Abram so they can obtain children from
her. Hagar brings forth a son, Ishmael. Now, you and I know that
taking things into our own hands when we walk with God never turns
out to be a good idea, causing the promises of God to be delayed. The
same goes for the actions of Abram and Sarai. Ishmael was born when
Abram was eighty-six and the Lord appears to Abram again when he is
ninety-nine, thirteen years later. This time God not only reminds
Abram of the covenant He made with him; the Almighty also changes
his name to Abraham.

Genesis 17:5(KJV) – Neither shall thy name any more be called
Abram, but thy name shall be Abraham; for a father of many
nations have I made thee.

God was saying that He had already made Abram what He called him
to be and from then on would identify him as such. From that point

forward, God referred to Abram as Abraham, which in Hebrew means 'father of a multitude'. Every time his new name is said either by him or by others, the promises of God for his life are being repeated and planted in his heart. The words of God's promise to Abraham had been spoken to him when he was seventy-five years old and Abraham was ninety-eight when God changed his name. It took twenty-four years for it to become real to Abram and for him to believe that he could be Abraham, the father of a multitude as God said.

The New Testament gives us a good example of God changing someone's name. One of the twelve disciples Jesus called was Simon, Andrew's brother. Jesus had gathered His disciples to the coast of Caesarea Philippi.

> Matthew 16:15-18(KJV) – He saith unto them, But whom say ye that I am? And Simon Peter answered and said, Thou art the Christ, the Son of the living God. And Jesus answered and said unto him, Blessed art thou, Simon Barjona: for flesh and blood hath not revealed it unto thee, but my Father which is in heaven. And I say also unto thee, That thou art Peter, and upon this rock I will build my church; and the gates of hell shall not prevail against it.

Jesus goes on to tell Peter that he will receive the keys to the kingdom of heaven, by which he will be able to lose and bind on earth as it is in heaven. This prophecy is probably as hard for Peter to believe as it was for Abraham to believe that his barren wife would give him a son. Simon's given name comes from a Hebrew word meaning 'to harken or to hear'. Now Jesus is changing His name to 'Peter', which in Greek means 'rock'. How many of you know that when you change the name of something, you change the way you perceive it? Jesus was speaking prophecy into Simon's life, prophesying what God had planned for this disciple. We know that sometimes the words that are spoken over us don't take root in our hearts, they don't stick. God had revealed to Simon by the Spirit who Jesus truly was, but four verses later, the disciple rebuked Jesus for telling them about what would happen to Him. Jesus, turning to Peter, says 'Get thee behind me, Satan'. Now Jesus had just changed the name of Simon, who received a revelation from God at that moment, to Peter. Then Peter takes his focus off the Spirit of God, Jesus Christ, standing before him and speaks through his carnal mind. Peter has returned to his 'Simon' nature with the 'Simon' way of thinking.

God calls you out of where you are, to abide in a new place with Him. He has spoken words into your life, promises that will come to pass. But beings that we walk in our carnal self, we can't wait for the timing of the Lord and we bring forth an Ishmael. When we see the errors of our way, it takes a bit to get our life on track with what God is doing. He can then repeat His vision for our life, reminding us of the name that He is calling us. He has named you 'redeemed' through the blood of Jesus Christ; you have been saved from sin and its penalties - Ephesians 1:7(KJV). Jesus 'blessed' us with all spiritual blessings in heavenly places in Christ - Ephesians 1:3(KJV). If we confess our sins, He is faithful and just to 'forgive' us our sins and to 'cleanse 'us from all unrighteousness - I John 1:9(KJV). He was wounded for our transgressions; He was bruised for our iniquities; the chastisement of our peace was upon Him; and with His stripes we are 'healed'-Isaiah 53:5(KJV). A good man obtaineth 'favour' of the Lord. - Proverbs 12:2a(KJV). Therefore, if any man be in Christ, he is a 'new creature': old things are passed away; behold, all things are become new. - II Corinthians 5:17(KJV)

Jesus told us in John 10 that He calls His sheep by name. That name is redeemed, blessed, forgiven, healed, favored, loved, cleansed, a new creature and many more. I will always be named Debbie by my physical appearance, but what am I called in my spirit? Do we walk through life identifying ourselves by names that are born out of our old carnal self? Or do we believe we are the names that Jesus has given to us, the ones He calls us by? The name with which you identify yourself, is it the name spoken by God for you or does it come from your past experiences? I encourage you to pray, voicing God's names for your life over yourself. Abraham and Peter were both reassured by the repeating of the changed name in their lives and you will be as well. Sit with Jesus and permit Him to reveal the names He is saying over your life. Allow Him to show you what He has placed inside of you. Don't meditate on those names that the enemy would say over you but on the names that Jesus is speaking and believe what is being spoken over your life, that it will manifest in the timing of the Lord. Believe that your name is redeemed, blessed, forgiven, healed, favored, loved, cleansed, and a new creature, but above all believe in the name of Jesus.

We give Him all praise and all glory.

50

Stripe

Stripe – a stroke or blow with a rod or lash

There are times in our walk with Jesus that we forget the price He paid for each of us; the agony and despair that He felt, the humiliation and degradation He suffered, knowing He would have to sacrifice Himself to fulfill the plan of God. We become so wrapped up in the affairs of this world that we fail to remember the cost He gave for our deliverance. When I started studying for this lesson, I was focusing on the stripes Isaiah prophesied concerning Jesus; saying that with His stripes, we are healed. Isaiah is speaking of the stripes as a result of Jesus being scourged. In Deuteronomy 25, under Mosaic law, it was forbidden to inflict more than forty stripes caused by flogging as punishment on an offender to prevent him from being publicly degraded. The instrument used for such punishments was generally made of calf leather divided into thongs with tips of metal or bone or shards of pottery. The damage done with this apparatus on the human body was to shred the flesh with each lash. Jesus was not sentenced before the Sanhedrin (a Jewish judicial body); so, the Jewish laws did not apply to Him. He was convicted in a Roman court before Pontius Pilate. The Roman Empire often used whipping and flogging as a preliminary to crucifixion, and the limit of no more than 40 lashes did not apply to them. Records in history tell of floggings of up to 100 lashes under Roman rule. There is no documentation in the Bible as to the number of stripes inflicted or the degree of injury that was done on Jesus, but it must have been intense.

> John 19:1(KJV) – Then Pilate therefore took Jesus, and scourged Him.

Pilate really tried to do the right thing by giving the Jews several chances to free Jesus, even telling them that he found no fault at all with Jesus. This was against the nature of Pilate, as he was described by historians to be a cruel, ruthless governor who knew how to do his job. Pilate ordered Jesus to be whipped like a criminal, in hopes of winning the crowd's sympathy and Jesus' release. Pilate was accustomed to giving orders and he could have had a Roman civil servant to do his bidding. Or the scripture says Pilate scourged Jesus; which could mean Pilate did the flogging himself; wanting to censor the amount of punishment inflicted on Jesus. And a second time, the ruler went out to the crowds of Jews and told them he had found no fault with Jesus. We have no way of knowing the degree that Jesus was scourged, but we know that Isaiah prophesied with Jesus' stripes we are healed.

> Isaiah 53:3-5(KJV) – He is despised and rejected of men; a man of sorrows, and acquainted with grief: and we hid as it were our faces from Him; He was despised, and we esteemed Him not. Surely, He hath borne our griefs, and carried our sorrows: yet we did esteem Him stricken, smitten of God, and afflicted. But He was wounded for our transgressions, He was bruised for our iniquities: the chastisement of our peace was upon Him; and with His stripes we are healed.

Isaiah foretold that the appearance of Jesus would not draw people to Him, that He would not have the stature of King Saul (who was over six feet tall) or be good-looking like King David (who had a handsome countenance). When they would see Jesus, they would not see beauty in His outer appearance; it would only be by the Spirit of God that they would see His inner beauty. So, He was shunned and discarded by most who came into contact with Him. But God had other plans for Jesus; because it was not an earthly king like Saul or David that God was sending, but the King of all kings. Isaiah tells in these scriptures that Jesus would be despised, hated, and rejected by those He came to save; which caused Him sorrow, because He could feel their pain. He knew if they would just accept Him, their suffering and despair could be taken away. Those who grew up in the spiritual legalism of the time would turn their backs on Jesus when He passed by and look the other way. Isaiah was prophesying to the children of Israel, who had been taught their whole lives about the coming of a Messiah; a Savior to rescue them from the oppressor. In Luke 24, Jesus explained thoroughly to the disciples all the scriptures concerning Himself from the beginning at Moses and all the prophets. So, there was plenty of documentation of His coming, but because He didn't come as they expected, they rejected Him. Isaiah told them this Savior would be afflicted with pain for their disobedience and wrongdoings. His physical body was beaten and bruised. He would become obedient to the death of the cross as a sacrifice for our transgressions and take the stripes of scourging for our healing. With His scourging, our assurance is that Jesus took away our sickness and diseases; putting them on Himself.

Have you ever tried to do something good for someone, only to be rejected and turned away? How many times has Jesus been there for you and you didn't even recognize Him? The Son of man is come to seek and to save the lost, and is snubbed; His sufferings being nothing. Of the many that have heard of the sacrifice Jesus made for them and profess to believe; few embrace it and submit to the power of it. Jesus loves each of us abundantly above what we can imagine, that He would come to earth as a man, walk among those who hated and despised Him, be rejected by those He encountered, and die as a sacrifice for all mankind's sins. He took our affliction on His body when he was beaten, bruised and scourged.

Don't get so wrapped up in your day-to-day life that you forget how blessed you are to have a Savior who gave it all for you. We have the assurance that no matter what comes against us, whatever affliction we go through, He has been there before. He has walked through it and He will be there to help us through. There is healing in His scars for every one of ours, with His stripes we are healed. There is power in Jesus; learn to walk in it. Remember all the things He did for you and believe for all He will do for you. Jesus is there for you when you need Him.

We give Him all praise and all glory.

51

Mind

Mind - the element of a person that enables them to be aware of the world and their experiences, to think, and to feel; the faculty of consciousness and thought:

When the Spirit of God spoke this word to me, I was familiar with several scriptures in the New Testament that referred to the 'mind', but not a one of them was brought to memory. During my daily Bible reading in I and II Corinthians, I began to take notice every time I read the word 'mind'. So, the teacher in me did a study on each occasion "mind' was used, not in the New Testament but just in the letters Paul wrote. I found that there were at least thirteen different Greek words that translated into the one English word 'mind'; much like the word 'love' that translates to four Greek words. In studying them out, I learned it was not a case of thirteen different minds, but that there were a variety of adjectives to describe our mind.

As I was writing this lesson, I looked out the window in front of me; onto the yard of the people that live across the street, noticing the four different trees they have in their yard. They are all trees, but there is a different adjective to describe each one. The first of the trees is a tall, mature weeping willow, which at this moment is gracefully blowing in the wind. Its branches are pliable making it easy for it to move toward the wind, but those same branches are prone to cracking or breaking under the weight of ice and snow buildup. Then there is a short crepe myrtle whose leaves are beginning to turn colors and fall off. During the summer months, this tree is covered with vibrant pink flowers, making it a beautiful addition to the landscape. It will not grow into a majestic shade cover for the yard, but will definitely add a variety of colors during its blooming season. The third tree is a live oak and just by looking at it you can tell it has weathered many harsh seasons in north Texas. This tree is drought resistant and can grow very tall and wide, but because it has not been pruned, it is growing unevenly and out of control. The final one is a Bradford pear tree, which is the youngest of all the trees. These trees grow fast and are pest-resistant/disease-free. It produces a fruit, but it is inedible and is poisonous to many animals.

As I was writing out the four trees with all of their traits, the Holy Spirit began to show me the similarities between them to our minds. First is the weeping willow tree; which compares to the mind of those who are not stable in their thinking. Paul wrote to the church at Ephesus.

Ephesians 4:14(KJV) - That we henceforth be no more children, tossed to and fro, and carried about with every wind of doctrine, by the sleight of men, and cunning craftiness, whereby they lie in wait to deceive.

This mind has not established itself in the power of walking in the mind of Christ, so every foolish doctrine or religious spirit causes it to be tossed. It believes everything it has been told, all that the liars or deceivers have said. Paul then goes on to say in Ephesians 4:17-18(KJV) -This I say therefore, and testify in the Lord, that ye henceforth walk not as other Gentiles walk, in the vanity of their mind, Having the understanding darkened, being alienated from the life of God through the ignorance that is in them, because of the blindness of their heart: Paul is telling them to not allow themselves to fall into following worthless pursuits, as those who are blind to true understanding in their mind and live in ignorance.

The second tree is the crepe myrtle which is very pretty to the eye, but because of its size, it gives no shade. It is content in its own mind to be the small, colorful tree in the group, with no aspirations to grow into what Jesus has for it. But we are told to be all that Jesus would have us to be; to increase in our knowledge of Him, become more faithful in our love for Him and our submission to Him. Paul wrote to the church in Philippi – Philippians 1:9-11(KJV) – And this I pray, that your love may abound yet more and more in knowledge and in all judgment; that ye may approve things that are excellent; that ye may be sincere and without offence till the day of Christ; being filled with the fruits of righteousness, which are by Jesus Christ, unto the glory and praise of God. Paul is praying to God for the church that they would grow in wisdom to determine the best from everything else. The enemy is whispering into the mind of the crepe myrtle that this is all you will ever be, this is all God will ever use you for. Paul is saying to pray that we should overflow with discernment to examine every thought that comes into our mind to determine whether it is righteous before God.

The live oak tree is the third one. It has been standing tall for a very long time, weathering seasons of lack and seasons of plenty. But now it doesn't know how much longer it can hold on; doubt and unbelief are creeping into its' mind. It has lost the attitude of praise that was its strength previously. As there has been no pruning on this tree, it has some areas that are very dense and other areas that the foliage is sparse. Jesus told us in John 15:2(KJV) – Every branch in me that beareth not fruit He taketh away: and every branch that beareth fruit, He purgeth it, that it may bring forth more fruit. This tree has not allowed the Holy Spirit to prune all the attitudes in the mind that hinder the production of those things it was created to bring forth. The mind of this tree is stifling the growth that allows it to be all that God plans for it to become and ends up being a scraggly mess.

The Bradford pear tree is standing out front all covered in pretty green leaves, but the fruit is worthless, it doesn't produce anything that is worthy. It works very hard to look good, making sure that it appears on the outside to all who see its beauty, that they won't notice that its fruit is insignificant. Paul wrote to the church in Philippi - Philippians 2:5-8(KJV) - Let this mind be in you, which was also in Christ Jesus: who, being in the form of God, thought it not robbery to be equal with God: but made Himself of no reputation, and took upon Him the form of a servant, and was made in the likeness of men: and being found in fashion as a man, He humbled Himself, and became obedient unto death, even the death of the cross. The Bradford pear should not allow its' mindset of being the pretty tree in the group to cloud its' need to bring forth fruit worthy of sharing. It needs to humble itself and allow the Spirit of God to use it. Paul is saying that we should adopt the mindset of Jesus, and not think so highly of ourselves. Jesus didn't stop being the Son of God. He didn't let His immortality stop Him from conveying humanity.

I Corinthians 2:16(KJV) – For who hath known the mind of the Lord, that he may instruct him? But we have the mind of Christ. Isaiah asked this same question to the children of Israel and at that time, no one knew the mind of God. We desire to think the way Jesus thinks, because He has the mind of God. Our prayer should be that the Father would let this mind be in me that was also in Christ Jesus. We do this by showing compassion for others as Jesus did. Don't put yourself first. Forget yourself long enough to help others.

Romans 12:2(KJV) – And be not conformed to this world; but be ye transformed by the renewing of your mind, that ye may prove what is that good, and acceptable, and perfect, will of God.

We give Him all praise and all glory.

52

Fear

Fear – a profound reverence and awe especially toward God

II Timothy 1:7 – For God hath not given us the spirit of fear; but of power, and of love, and of a sound mind.

Paul wrote this letter to Timothy, his son in the faith. We first read about the relationship between Paul and Timothy in Act 16, when Timothy starts following Paul in his missionary journeys. Timothy spent years traveling with Paul to various cities, preaching the gospel of Jesus Christ and setting up churches for those who believed. Their relationship grew over time and toward the end of Paul's life in prison, he wrote to Timothy encouraging him to remember the genuine faith that is in him and to stir up the gift of God which was placed in him by the laying on of Paul's hands. Timothy was in Ephesus when Paul wrote him this letter, dealing with the issues that were common in the early church, which included false teachers and trying to bring order in the assembly by qualified elders and deacons. Although Timothy was quite a bit younger than Paul, he was thrown into the fire of the church at Ephesus because he was gifted, called and well equipped. In this scripture, the word 'fear' translates to the Greek to mean timid or easily frightened. Paul is reminding Timothy that the indwelling of the

Holy Spirit does not make you timid or easily frightened. Rather, the Holy Spirit within Timothy gives him 'dunamis' power, the strength and ability to stand in the assembly with confidence that is not in him by nature. Also, Timothy is filled with the 'agape' love for his brothers in Christ, not allowing the spirit of condemnation to come for those who are attacking the church. Timothy is reminded that it is this love that is kind and patient; that will draw others to the body of Christ. Finally, Timothy is told that God gave him a sound mind, which translates the discipline of self-control, the ability to influence those that are put in his charge with the word of God. Breaking the scripture down – The indwelling of the Holy Spirit does not cause you to be timid or afraid. He does not leave you without comfort. By having the indwelling of the Holy Spirit with evidence of speaking in tongues, you are given gifts to use that God has for you to walk in His strength, to have the love for others that God has for you and the discipline, the self-control that comes from being in the presence of God. When you are walking in this place with God, there is no room for you to be afraid or timid, no room for the spirit of fear.

> Romans 8:14-15 – For as many as are led by the Spirit of God, they are the sons of God. For ye have not received the spirit of bondage again to fear; but ye have received the Spirit of adoption, whereby we cry, Abba, Father.

The children of Israel know all about the spirit of bondage. Their ancestors were slaves under the Egyptian rule during the time of Moses. With the instructions from Moses who was led by God, the Israelites were freed of bondage by the order of the pharaoh. Then came the hard part. Moses led them out into the wilderness with only a cloud by day and a fire by night to guide them. Do you ever feel like God is leading you by the light of a candle and you don't know what is up ahead, if there are any pitfalls or enemies who will harm you? The

Israelites felt that way causing, them to murmur and complain the entire time Moses led them. In Deuteronomy 1, Moses gives an explanation to the current generation of Israelites of what God has done for their parents. This group is the children who were born in the wilderness of the original exiles; all the original exiles had died by now. Moses told the older generation of exiles that God said they had been in the wilderness long enough and now was the time to take the Amorite territory.

> Deuteronomy 1:21 – Behold, the Lord thy God hath set the land before thee: go up and possess it, as the Lord God of thy fathers hath said unto thee; fear not, neither be discouraged.

When the people heard the instructions from God, they came to Moses and said 'Maybe we should send a group of men to search out the land and bring back word of how they should take control of the land'. They didn't listen to the word of the Lord who said, 'Go up and possess the land; fear not, neither be discouraged'. God had already gone before them and made a way, but they chose not to believe it. They allowed the spirit of fear to come over them; so they sent a group of twelve men to spy out the land. The spies came back with a good report, telling the children of Israel that it was a wonderful land that God was going to give them. God didn't instruct the Israelites to go fight the Amorites, He told them to go to the land and take possession of it. They felt the need to take up arms and go to battle with the Amorites. Does the spirit of fear cause you to feel the need to add to what God has told you to do, to try to enhance God's instructions because you think you know better? God told them that they didn't have to fight this battle themselves. He would always go before them; just like when He brought them out of Egypt and delivered them all the way across the wilderness. He would deliver them now before the Amorites. But the children of Israel didn't believe it and now the Lord was very angry with them, telling them not a single one of this wicked generation will see the promise land. The results of the children of Israel acting on the spirit of fear caused what originally was to be an eleven-day journey to turn into forty years of wandering in the wilderness.

What is God telling you to go up and possess in your life? Is there a promised land He has waiting for you and all you have to do is pray through the spirit of fear that is trying to keep you out of your birthright? Can you just look past your fears to see the promise land God has for you – to see the bigger picture? With all this study on the fear that is not of God, there is a fear that each of us should have; that is the fear of the Lord.

> Matthew 10:28 – And fear not them which kill the body, but are not able to kill the soul: but rather fear Him which is able to destroy both soul and body in hell.

We are all faced with fears at one time or another in our lives. It is what we do with them that makes a difference. Take your eyes off whatever fear is causing you to focus on and look to Jesus, the author and finisher of our faith.

We give Him all praise and all Glory.

53

❦

Walk

Walk – *to move along on foot*

We make decisions every day, all day long, regarding actions in our life. When we wake up, we decide whether to get up or just stay in bed for more sleep. Do you pray before you start your day that your footsteps be ordered by the Lord, that He would lead you in the path He has for you for that day? Or do you jump out of bed, full steam ahead, making decisions for yourself about what you should do during the day? If you would allow God to order your steps, and lead you in the way you should go, you will have a more peaceable journey.

> Psalms 37:23 – The steps of a good man are ordered by the LORD; and he delighteth in his way.

King David is writing in this psalm that if you, as a righteous man or woman, would allow God to order your steps, He will strengthen you in the course of the journey. In doing so, God delights in each step you take, blessing your path. You are pleasing to Him. In the natural, walking has become a popular exercise for us. Some of the benefits include maintaining a healthy weight, strengthening bones and muscles, increasing energy levels, and reducing stress and tension. The result is a stronger body, that is able to ward off attacks of sickness and disease, but the strength doesn't come overnight. You start with a routine of getting out a few minutes a day, and walking a short distance. Then you increase the amount of time you walk and the distance you go. If you happen to miss a day, you don't give up because you can see such a transformation in you. These same benefits apply when you walk in the Spirit. Your spirit is strengthened each time you take a step. Stress and tension fall off because you have allowed the Holy Spirit to lead you in making decisions. You also find the power of the Holy Spirit is greater in your life. All it takes is lifting one foot up and setting it down in faith; not permitting the things around you to influence you. In your walk with God, you start out going to Him each day with the big things, the major decisions. Then, as you increase your walk in Him, you get stronger in the spirit and begin to see a transformation in your spiritual life.

II Corinthians 5:7 – (For we walk by faith, not by sight:)

Paul is writing to the church, reminding us not to look at the external appearance, but to allow the Holy Spirit to be our guide as we progress in our spiritual growth. Each step you walk is a step of faith. You are walking out of the past into what God wants to do in your life. But sometimes we don't want to let go of the past, in order to take the steps God is desiring for our lives. What keeps you from trusting to walk with God in the present is what you are attached to in the past.

In John chapter 5, it is written that Jesus went to Jerusalem during the time of a Jewish feast. There He came upon a pool with five covered porches surrounding it. This pool was a gathering place for a great multitude of people who were blind, lame (unable to walk), and withered (paralyzed). The attraction to the pool was that at a certain season, a messenger from God would come down and stir the water. The first afflicted person to make it into the pool was made whole of whatever disease he had. There was a certain man there, who had feebleness in his body for thirty-eight years. John 5:6(KJV) – When Jesus saw him lie, and knew that he had been there a long time in that case, He saith unto him, "Wilt thou be made whole?" The Lord didn't ask him if he wanted to be healed. He asked if the man wanted to be made whole. There is a distinction between these two conditions. Healing meant that he would be free of the paralyzing disease in his physical body. But to be made whole means that not only is the physical body healed but also you are developing a deeper commitment to God, with a more constant mindfulness of the indwelling of the Holy Spirit. I am not saying that we shouldn't pray to be healed; but when you walk in divine health, you are walking in His Spirit. The paralyzed man explained that each time the water was troubled, he tried to get to it, but someone else stepped down before him. How many times when God is moving in our lives do we give Him an excuse why it won't work? The man at the pool told Jesus that he tried, BUT. However, we serve a God that is bigger than our excuse.

John 5:8 – Jesus saith unto him, Rise, take up thy bed, and walk.

The Greek word for 'rise' means to move from sitting to standing up. Jesus told him to stand; but didn't leave him with only that instruction. He also told him to take up his bed. Jesus is saying, 'Don't look back from where you came'. Then He instructed the man to 'Walk'. The man had not walked for thirty-eight years, so I am sure it took a great step of faith and trust on his part to even make the first move. Over a long period of non-use, the muscles in the man's legs had grown weak;

but were made strong by the word of Jesus. How often do we give Jesus an excuse for not changing from the condition we are in? When was the last time He told you to 'Rise' out of your situation and 'Take up thy bed" so there is no place for you to go back and 'Go Forth' in what He has for you? Take that first step by putting your trust in Jesus; having faith that He will lead you. Your faith will increase with each step you take and soon you will be walking and dancing with the indwelling of the Holy Spirit to guide you.

In going through a notebook from years ago, I came across this word from Jesus that applies to each of us as we learn to walk out what God has for us.

The walk you have been called for is not easy. But I am here for you; I love you. All you have to do is draw My living water from My well. It will refresh you in your weariness. It will give you strength for the battles. Thus saith the Lord Jesus.

Each step in your walk is a step of faith, a progressive revelation. It's not going to be easy. Walk out of the past into what God wants to do in your life. What keeps you from trusting God in the present is what you are attached to in the past. Let the things of this world, the lust of the flesh, the lust of the eyes, and the pride of life fall away. Trust Him enough to take the first step; and continue to trust Him to keep stepping. Each time you take a step, go to God and allow Him to show you the way. It is not how fast you walk or how far you walk, but the consistency of putting one foot in front of the other and always having one foot on the ground (always being grounded in Him). Not walking with Him, but walking "in" Him. My desire is to walk in all the things the Father has for me – both in the spiritual and in the natural.

We give Him all praise and all glory.

54

Sacrifice

Sacrifice – *surrendering a possession an act of offering to God*

It is estimated that 45 million Americans go on a diet each year and that they spend $33 billion a year on weight loss products. Research suggests that approximately eighty percent of those who have a major weight loss will regain the weight in the next twelve months. Most of us at one time or another have been on a diet, whether it be a food intake modification or dietary supplements. At some point, you might begin to feel deprived of the foods you enjoy and that you are having to make too great a sacrifice. This causes you to have the desire to cheat, which produces unappealing results on the scale. But flesh wants what flesh wants. What price are you willing to pay to eat comfort food? If we would just learn to obey what the Holy Spirit prompts us to eat, instead of sacrificing, as the world would have us do, maybe we would be able to see success. Our heavenly Father knew that obedience would be tougher to accomplish than a mere sacrifice.

The Bible is full of instances where God has proclaimed His plan to His people and instead of obeying; they did what was right in their own eyes. They thought that a sacrifice to God would appease the Almighty as an alternative to obedience. Saul was the first king anointed to rule over the children of Israel. While he was king, he had been given great victories over their enemies. The prophet Samuel tells King Saul that the Lord is going to punish the Amalekites because they ambushed the Israelites in their path out of Egypt. The instruction given from God to Saul was to destroy everything, all the men, women, children, ox and sheep, camel and donkey. However, Saul decided not to follow all the instructions exactly as they came from God, instead, he did just what was convenient for himself. He kept the best of the sheep and livestock; and also captured the king of the Amalekites; only destroying what was of poor quality or worthless to him. But God saw the king's actions differently and judged him for those deeds. When Samuel received a message from God for the king, he went looking for Saul and was told Saul had gone to Carmel.

> I Samuel 15:12 – And when Samuel rose early to meet Saul in the morning, it was told Samuel, saying, Saul came to Carmel, and, behold, he set him up a place, and is gone about, and passed on, and gone down to Gilgal.

Samuel is told that the king had been in Carmel and while he was there, he set up a place for himself. Saul erected a tribute, a memorial, a 'place' which in Hebrew translates to mean ' a hand, an open one indicating power'. Saul was so proud and confident of his actions with the Amalekites that he wanted to commemorate his victory. I am sure the prophet was infuriated with the king because God had told Samuel because of the results of Saul's choices, he would no longer be king and Samuel was to deliver the message to Saul. When Samuel finally found the king, Saul had no idea that his actions had caused anger from the Heavenly Father. The prophet questioned Saul concerning the reason he didn't obey the voice of God. Saul told him 'I did as the Lord commanded', it was the people who took the sheep and cattle from the spoils to sacrifice to God.

> I Samuel 15:22 – And Samuel said, Hath the LORD as great delight in burnt offerings and sacrifices, as in obeying the voice of the LORD? Behold, to obey is better than sacrifice, and to hearken than the fat of rams.

Samuel is asking Saul does he think that God delights more in sacrifices and burnt offerings as much as He delights in perfect obedience to His voice. Saul recognizes he has been caught and still blames the people by saying he was afraid of them and that is what kept him from obeying God. We have a saying in our household – I don't want to hear the labor pains, I just want to see the baby. God didn't care what reason Saul did what he did, all God wanted was obedience to His commands. Saul should have read up on his history and taken a note from his ancestor, Abraham. God gave Abraham a test that we all hope we don't have to experience. The Almighty told him to take his son, his only son, and offer him for a burnt offering. Abraham did exactly as God said to the point of putting his son on the altar and picking up the knife. The angel of the Lord called out of heaven to Abraham.

> Genesis 22:12 – And he said, Lay not thine hand upon the lad, neither do thou anything unto him: for now I know that thou fearest God, seeing thou hast not withheld thy son, thine only son from Me.

Abraham was willing to obey God and sacrifice Isaac, a type and shadow of Jesus Christ. God knew what He was asking of Abraham, as the Almighty would someday give His Son as a sacrifice. God knew that Abraham feared and respected the one True God and would be faithful to follow His commands, because he was willing to give to God that which was most precious to him. Just as God knew Abraham's heart concerning Isaac, He also knew Saul's heart. Saul was more concerned with being king and all the attention and accolades that came with it, than with fearing God.

When was the last time God requested something from you that was very precious, an item that you treasured? You may not have given it directly to God, but He spoke into your life with directions to give your precious item away. Were you obedient to obey God or did you hold on to your treasure? Sacrifice or obedience? Which will it be?

> II Corinthians 10:5-6 – Casting down imaginations, and every high thing that exalteth itself against the knowledge of God, and bringing into captivity every thought to the obedience of Christ; And having in a readiness to revenge all disobedience, when your obedience is fulfilled.

Obedience is a change of the heart, making it more Christ-like. Abraham never thought at the birth of Isaac that someday, he would be standing on a mountain, giving back to God the greatest blessing he would receive in his lifetime; but Abraham had faith in God. Isaac was the promised seed that God had foretold to Abraham and Sarah, the son they had prayed for and believed in God for. Abraham had to believe in his heart that God's will would be done and that the Almighty would provide what is needful for His will. Maturity in God is when we willingly offer to God whatever He asks of us, no matter how great or how small. It is not the sacrifice God is looking for in our lives, but our obedience to Him and submission to His will. To obey is better than sacrifice.

We give Him all praise and all glory.

About Author

I am Debra Albrecht. Fifteen years ago, a very perceptive pastor could see the gift and calling of teaching on my life. I watched the hand of the Lord in each step of the growth process, line upon line, here a little, there a little. I started out speaking a sentence or two in the church service, which led to God prompting me to write out a short message and email it to a few members of the church. The email list grew and so did the content. Each week God speaks a single word into my spirit and I put those words down pen to paper; writing all that He speaks. It is my faith in God that has kept me writing devotedly each week, my obedience to His calling in my life all of these years, hearing God's voice to write what He said, and humbleness of spirit to give God all the credit for the book. My heart is to write words that the Holy Spirit will open the meaning of the Word of God to all those who read the book.

Made in the USA
Monee, IL
09 December 2023

48718462R00131